AF557816

THE DECEPTION INDUSTRY

THE DECEPTION INDUSTRY

The **Art**, **Craft** and **Science** of **HACKING THE ELECTORATE**

HERJINDER

RUPA

First published by
Rupa Publications India Pvt. Ltd 2024
7/16, Ansari Road, Daryaganj
New Delhi 110002

Sales centres:
Bengaluru Chennai
Hyderabad Jaipur Kathmandu
Kolkata Mumbai Prayagraj

P-ISBN: 978-93-6156-218-1
E-ISBN: 978-93-6156-823-7

First impression 2024

10 9 8 7 6 5 4 3 2 1

Printed in India

CONTENTS

CONTENTS

PROLOGUE

We were kids who had just learnt to read and write. Aside from school books, we attempted to read and comprehend whatever came our way—whether it was a nameplate outside someone's house, a shop's signboard or leaflets handed at road intersections. At the time, like in the rest of the Hindi heartland, a unique sort of leaflet was distributed in and around Lucknow every four to six months. These were known as '*Santoshi Mata ka parcha* (Pamphlet of Santoshi Mata)'. It was sometimes a story featuring Santoshi Mata, and at times a story of another local deity.

This story, written in Hindi, summarized below, was quite engaging. It went as such:

> *A snake appeared in a village as a farmer was ploughing his field. Before the farmer could do anything, the snake said, 'Don't be afraid, and pay close attention to what I'm saying. I've been sent to you by the Goddess to tell you the truth. The Goddess's glory is spreading quickly all around, and during this time, those who become devotees of the Goddess will have luck on their side, while those who do not will face the Goddess's wrath. You will quickly see positive effects if you print and distribute leaflets in favour of the Goddess.'*
>
> *The farmer got two hundred pamphlets with the full narrative printed and circulated them, and the next day he discovered gold buried in his field and became wealthy. When another farmer from a nearby village distributed similar pamphlets, he won the first prize in the lottery ticket he had bought. When a government employee kept putting*

it off, his son was bitten by a snake and died as a result. When a shopkeeper ripped up such a pamphlet and called it a fabrication, he went bankrupt and got leprosy.

Nowadays, when media experts examine fake news appearing on social media, they describe its quality as 'crafted for circulation'[1]. That is, its composition makes individuals feel compelled to forward it. But, as we can see from the story of the Santoshi Mata leaflet, this craft for circulation is not new; it has been used for ages.

Many devout people would avoid reading or even touching such pamphlets when they were distributed. They feared that if they read it, it would necessitate the printing and distribution. Many individuals rejected it as a hoax and dismissed it totally. It was also referred to as a 'printing press conspiracy' by some. After reading such pamphlets, just a few people would get them printed and disseminated, thereby continuing the process of circulation. If we are to believe that printing and distributing leaflets like this was the ultimate goal, we must also acknowledge that the success rate of these pamphlets was quite low.

The same thing also happened with the election campaigns of that era. The entire campaign was built around the concept of 'one shoe fits all'. A vast quantity of election leaflets were made and distributed. These leaflets catered to a diverse range of people: those willing to vote for the respective party, those not willing to vote for the party and even those who may decide not to vote at all. They even reached out to individuals who were not yet eligible to vote. Similarly, the publicity done through the mike and loudspeaker was for everyone; all types of audiences were assembled in rallies, and door-to-door campaigns were carried out by knocking on the doors of every house in all localities. All of these techniques of communication had the same success percentage as Santoshi Mata's leaflets.

---

[1]Varis, Piia, *Conspiracy Theorising Online*, Tilburg University, 2019.

However, in the last few years, technology has completely transformed this. Election campaigns are finally free of the one-size-fits-all limitation. It is now quite simple and viable to ensure that your message reaches only the person you want it to reach, while their neighbour might receive an entirely different message. A significant number of people ingest the entire political narrative on handheld devices. Now, any type of propaganda can be distributed directly to the public.

Back then, not more than two to four types of leaflets could be distributed to voters in a constituency during an election. However, you can now send thousands of tailored messages to meet the expectations of the voter segment you are targeting. The sheer quantity of messaging has also influenced the quality of the election campaigns. We don't even know who sends these texts.

Previously, most of those who campaigned were visible to us, came to our neighbourhood and met us. But now, backroom boys are in charge of a big part of the electoral campaign. They are not discussed on television news channels, and their activities are not reported in newspapers. As a result, the elections of the new era frequently appear mysterious.

This book is simply an attempt to comprehend and solve this mystery.

PART ONE

BASIC TOOLS

1

THE GIZMO THAT ALTERED THE GAME

For India, the 1990s were an era of high aspirations. The balance-of-payments problem at the outset of the decade convinced both India's elite and middle class that it was time to change course. The Indian society was eager to break numerous restraints that kept it from walking with the rest of the globe. People were certain that economic policies laden with socialist jargon could no longer lead the country forward. When P.V. Narasimha Rao became the prime minister (PM) in 1991, he was determined to make a difference. Pandit Sukh Ram, a Member of Parliament (MP), from Himachal Pradesh's Mandi Lok Sabha constituency, was a key member of Rao's Cabinet. Sukh Ram was the union minister of state, communications (independent charge). When the then Finance Minister Manmohan Singh was sitting in New Delhi's North Block, pushing hard for economic liberalization, Sukh Ram was sitting in Sanchar Bhawan, just a short distance away, leaving no stone unturned to liberalize the communication sector.[1]

Landline phones arrived in India long before Independence. These phones remained status symbols for over a half a century after Independence. However, the number of landline connections was not growing at the same pace as the people moving upward

[1]Grewal Sharma, Manraj, 'Sukh Ram (1927-2022): The Man Who Rang in Telecom Revolution, Could Never Wash off Scam Taint', *The Indian Express*, 12 May 2022, http://tinyurl.com/ybhfby6y. Accessed on 13 February 2024.

or making progress. It used to take a year from the time an application for a new phone line was submitted to the time the phone was delivered. It took significantly longer in certain places. Industrialists and journalists would go to the communications minister's house to get an out-of-turn phone connection. Every MP had a quota of two out-of-turn phone connections per year. Thus, there was always a mob of phone connection seekers at their residence. During the time of scarcity, some back doors were built and opened exclusively for persons with significant connections. In any case, the need outnumbered the availability.

Early in Sukh Ram's tenure, landline service was substantially expanded. Public call offices (PCOs) were set up in every street and nook, allowing people to call someone in any corner of the world. Long-distance phone calls became increasingly reliable and convenient as technology advanced. Most importantly, long distance call rates were significantly cut. As a result, PCOs started doing good business. There used to be quite a crowd outside PCOs after 10.00 p.m., when call prices were lowered to one-fourth.

The rapid growth of the waiting list for phone connections suggested that the telephone was becoming a need as the economy and society changed. However, the government was unable to meet the demand. It was not easy to set up telephone infrastructure throughout the country. Even in cities and towns where it was previously installed, the system was not adequate enough to meet the needs of the population. It was unthinkable for every village in the country to have phone connectivity.

It was clear that rather than needing to arrange for cables and wires to be brought everywhere, connectivity across India could be more easily accomplished through mobile phone networks. But this was not an easy task. Mobile phone networks meant privatization and that signified the end of the government's monopoly in the communications industry. The trade unions in that sector were steadfast in their opposition. Despite the fact that the country's middle class was totally in favour of it, the political

Opposition was also not in favour of the proposal. They contended that because communication is a sensitive industry, permitting the private sector to assist and seeking a helping hand from foreign technologies and firms would jeopardize the country's security.

But nothing was going to stop the government from liberalizing. When the government unveiled its communication policy in 1994, plans were made to open up a slew of new avenues. Eight companies had been granted licences to launch mobile services in the four major cities of Delhi, Bombay (now Mumbai), Madras (now Chennai) and Calcutta (now Kolkata). Applications for mobile phone connections flooded in quickly.[2]

THE GAME CHANGER

Generally, it is difficult to pinpoint a single date for a significant societal change. However, in India, one such significant change across society does have a specific date. We know exactly when it all began.

It happened on a beautiful afternoon on 31 July 1995.[3] This date is now indelibly etched in Indian history. India made its first mobile call on that day. Jyoti Basu, the then chief minister (CM) of West Bengal, called Sukh Ram, the then union communications minister. The call was made from a Nokia phone, and the company that launched the mobile phone service was Modi Telstra.[4]

It was a highly publicized event. The news was all over the place. Newspapers published editorials on the topic, along with a variety of commentaries. High hopes were established by business associations and industry organizations.

---

[2]Singh Bedi, Navjot, *RF Spectrum Allocation Process in India*, Centre for Joint Warfare Studies, 2019.

[3]'25 Years of Mobility in India: The First Mobile Phone Call Was Made on This Day', *HTTech*, 20 August 2022, http://tinyurl.com/4crc2xua. Accessed on 13 February 2024.

[4]Ibid.

Every time a new technology has arrived in India, we have seen the same level of enthusiasm. However, in this case what came after it was launched and how it got domesticated was more important than the initial enthusiasm.

Initially, mobile phones were prohibitively expensive. Where previously a landline phone was considered a luxury, mobile phones entered as a super luxury. It was more of a status symbol than a communication instrument back then. Having a mobile phone indicated that you came from an affluent background. Not just the mobile phones, but even the services were pricey. A call from a mobile phone cost several times as more than a call from a landline. Similarly, there were charges for receiving mobile phone calls as well. A popular joke back then was that if you sold one of your kidneys to buy a cell phone, your other kidney would soon be sold to pay the monthly bill. This barrier, however, did not last long.

Shortly after, on an evening in 1996, the Central Bureau of Investigation (CBI) raided Sukh Ram's homes and offices and recovered a large sum of money.[5] After an investigation, it was found that, at a time when privatization and liberalization of telecom services were desperately required, money and shady activities were playing a significant role in the privatization process. While Sukh Ram will always be credited for laying the groundwork for India's communication revolution, the CBI raid tainted not only his image but the entire process of the liberalization of the communication sector. One of the poster boys for liberalization had become tarnished. Though this did not mark the end of his political career, he was never able to achieve similar stature again.

What happened to Modi Telstra was much worse. This service provider's run was short. Modi Telstra, a subsidiary of

---

[5]Grewal Sharma, Manraj, 'Sukh Ram (1927-2022): The Man Who Rang in Telecom Revolution, Could Never Wash off Scam Taint', *The Indian Express*, 12 May 2022, http://tinyurl.com/ybhfby6y. Accessed on 13 February 2024.

the Bhupendra Kumar Modi Group, was the first to receive a 'Certificate of Quality' from the Telecom Engineering Commission for Cellular Service, but it was not a commercial success. Afterwards, it sold its entire business to Idea Cellular, and no one recalls Modi Telstra anymore.[6]

As mentioned earlier, India's first mobile phone call was made using a Nokia phone. It was dominating the global mobile phone market at the time. It cashed in as soon as it hit the Indian market. For a long time, Nokia remained synonymous with good mobile phones. Following its initial success in India, Nokia decided to establish a mobile phone manufacturing plant in Tamil Nadu.[7] However, technology was rapidly changing, and this Finnish corporation was unable to keep up. Simultaneously, Nokia suffered from a series of disastrous decisions, and its share in the mobile phone market fell sharply. It later entered the market by incorporating new technology, but it subsequently lost its allure. Today, if any two leaders decided to make a first mobile phone call, like Jyoti Basu and Sukh Ram had, the phone they use would most likely not be a Nokia.

MOBILE MANIA GRIPS THE COUNTRY

Sociologists regard mobile phones as a disruptive technology. This technology has advanced at the expense of all established beliefs, customs and even systems. It has changed the way people communicate, acquire information and interact with everything they encounter daily.

---

[6]In 2017, Idea bought Spice Telecom; 'Idea-Spice Deal 4th Largest M&A in India', *DNA*, 15 September 2017, http://tinyurl.com/4abrcfd9. Accessed on 13 February 2024.

[7]Das, Goutam, and N. Madhavan, 'Death of a Dream: The Rise and Fall of Nokia's Chennai Factory', *BTMAG*, 17 August 2014, http://tinyurl.com/yvsa6pxe. Accessed on 13 February 2024.

When Atal Bihari Vajpayee's government took office at the Centre, a new communication policy was put into effect. Following this, call rates began to fall. In the meantime, mobile phone firms realized that offering low-cost service to millions of people may be more profitable than providing high-cost service to a few lakh individuals; the market had matured. While mobile service providers used to charge ₹10 for a 30-second call in 1996, by 2003 it had dropped to less than ₹1.[8]

The new communication policy also paved the way for the mobile network to grow beyond the metropolises. Soon after, mobile network towers began to appear in towns, villages and even hilly and tribal areas. They quickly spread to places where the roads were not even properly constructed. Mobile phones were also introduced in communities where there was no reliable power supply. The business of charging phones with batteries had already begun in such places. A big portion of India leapfrogged to the mobile phone era without having seen the telegraph, landline phones, phonograph, fax or pager.

By 2004, the number of mobile phones in the country had surpassed the number of landline phones.[9] Mobile phones became less expensive than a bicycle.[10] However, the majority of the low-cost phones were first-generation Chinese models with ambiguous quality. But the best part was that for the first time, people had such an affordable choice that gave them a facility that had previously only been available to the upper class.

---

[8]'From Rs 24 for a Call to the Lowest Rates in the World', *The Times of India*, 4 August 2020, http://tinyurl.com/4vrtusxy. Accessed on 13 February 2024.

[9]Chatterjee, Abhishek, 'India's Mobile Revolution Turns 25: Tracking the High and Low Points', *The Hindu*, 22 October 2020, http://tinyurl.com/njpcenbh. Accessed on 13 February 2024.

[10]Doron, Assa, and Robin Jeffrey, 'Celling India: Exploring a Society's Embrace of the Mobile Phone', *South Asian History and Culture*, Vol. 2, No. 3, July 2011, pp. 397–416.

There was nothing that could stop the march of the mobile phone after that. In the four years that followed, the number of mobile phones in the country surpassed all previous records. There were more than 300 million mobile phone connections in the country at the time. That equates to approximately 30 mobile phones for every 100 individuals. This figure was higher than the daily newspaper circulation in India at the time. After China, India had become the world's second largest mobile phone market.[11]

This figure was something to be proud of, but another figure that followed afterwards was not a proud moment for the country. According to reports, the number of mobile phones in the country had surpassed the number of toilets.[12] The irony is not lost. Mobile phones became more important than a basic human need.

Prior to mobile phones, the villagers had become acquainted with technology such as radio and television. These technological products were highly public in nature, but the mobile phone was infiltrating everyone's personal space. It had the advantage of not requiring a constant supply of electricity. The most significant advantage was that no exceptional technical knowledge was required to utilize it. Even those who couldn't read could suddenly communicate with anyone with very little effort.

The devices that were once only seen in the hands of the urban elite, had now penetrated every village. It was no longer a strange item even for people from far-flung places. Soon, the mobile phone became such a mainstream accessory of the nation that everyone wanted to join, even the ones who had been trying unsuccessfully

---

[11]Singh, Sanjay Kumar, 'The Diffusion of Mobile Phones in India', *Telecommunications Policy*, Vol. 32, No. 9–10, 2008, pp. 642–51.

[12]'Greater Access to Cell Phones than Toilets in India: UN', *United Nations University*, 14 April 2015, http://tinyurl.com/5n6wehmd. Accessed on 13 February 2024.

for years to demonstrate that they were not part of the mainstream.[13]

A NEW ERA IN INDIAN POLITICS

The widespread use of mobile phones began to alter society in every aspect. It began to benefit everyone, from great businessmen to little traders and even artisans. The economy was expanding, and mobile phones were playing an essential role in the new opportunities that were emerging. The changes brought about by this were numerous and far-reaching, but for the time being, we shall limit ourselves to the changes brought about in Indian politics as a result of mobile phones.

As mentioned previously, when mobile phones initially became available in towns and villages, it remained in the hands of those we refer to as the 'power elite'. These are people linked with power, particularly power politics. Mobile phones gradually reached village leaders as well as workers from numerous political parties. Owing to this, several villages were able to emerge from their relative isolation. As a result, their communication with higher-ranking leaders grew, resulting in a rise in their activism. It was also easier for those leaders to communicate with each village. In addition, mobile phones linked these villages in real time to the narratives being developed at the national and state levels. It was at this point that a major rejuvenation began in Indian politics.

Previously, it was quite difficult to send messages to remote villages. Politicians had to frequently deploy messengers to convey any information. These messengers used to travel there by bus, cycle, bullock cart and so on. Snail mail was sometimes used for this, albeit there was no guarantee of when it would reach. Kanshi Ram, the founder of the Bahujan Samaj Party (BSP), is claimed

---

[13]For example, there were various extremist groups in the Northeast that were keen to adopt mobile telephone when it arrived in India.

to have used telegrams to transmit messages and structured his entire organization around it.[14] Remote areas in Uttar Pradesh (UP) and Punjab, where he was laying the foundations for his party, could be accessed in this manner. It is also worth noting that the organization from which this entire party arose was the Post and Telegraph Department's labour union.

In the 2004 general elections, the Bharatiya Janata Party (BJP) was the first to employ mobile phones for electoral campaigning. The phones across the country abruptly rang, and upon connecting, a voice came, 'Namaskar, I am Atal Bihari Vajpayee'. He was the country's PM at the time, and he was campaigning for the next term. He used this pre-recorded phone call to urge folks to vote for his party. There were 72 million such phone calls made, including 46 million to landlines and 26 million to mobile phones.[15]

It is a different story that his appeal had little impact and that his party did not receive enough votes to form a government. However, when the then Gujarat CM Narendra Modi used the same strategy during the Assembly elections three years later, he got a huge success.

The divergent outcomes of these two cases demonstrated that a mobile phone is merely a medium, and elections are not won only on the basis of a communication medium. Victory requires a narrative that can sway the majority of voters. Whatever the outcome, Indian politicians had found a way to speak directly to the voters through the mobile phone.

The 2007 Legislative Assembly elections in UP was most likely the first-time mobile phone connectivity exhibited its true political

---

[14]Doron, Assa, and Robin Jeffrey, *The Great Indian Phone Book: How the Cheap Cell Phone Changes Business, Politics, and Daily Life*, Harvard University Press, 2013.

[15]Willnat, Lars, and Annette Aw, 'Elections in India: One Billion People and Democracy', *The Handbook of Election Coverage around the World*, Jesper Strömbäck and Lynda Lee Kaid (eds), Lawrence Erlbaum, 2009, pp. 123–40.

potential. The number of mobile phone connections in UP had surpassed 3 crore by the time this election took place. That is, one phone for every six or seven persons.[16] It was called 'India's first mass mobile phone election'.[17]

For the BSP, this election was not easy as the party's major constituency was Dalit voters. Most of these voters could not be reached through mobile phones because the state's Dalit community had the lowest mobile phone density. However, BSP prevailed in the election by craftily using whatever mobile connectivity they had. And that decidedly paid off.

The party made sure that the grassroots organization was connected to Dalit workers who owned mobile phones. Many party members, including those in the rural, were now in constant contact with the party's top leaders. Mobile phones had established a dependable arrangement that anytime a leader of the party visited a village seeking votes, the residents of the area would be alerted of his arrival well in advance.

The entire voting process in UP election took about a month. The polling took place in seven phases, and the party assigned the roles of 'booth in charge' and 'booth employee' only to people who owned a mobile phone. This greatly aided in maintaining constant surveillance until polling time. The news of any election misconduct anywhere reached the leaders in real time, and they were also able to provide an immediate remedy to the situation.

When the results came in, the game had completely changed. The BSP had won 206 of the state's 403 Assembly seats.[18] Previously,

---

[16]Doron, Assa, and Robin Jeffrey, *The Great Indian Phone Book: How the Cheap Cell Phone Changes Business, Politics, and Daily Life*, Harvard University Press, 2013.

[17]Ibid.

[18]PTI, 'Uttar Pradesh Assembly Elections: "BSP Will Repeat 2007 Victory," Says Mayawati', *Firstpost,* 19 February 2022, http://tinyurl.com/bdev739m. Accessed on 13 February 2024.

party leader Mayawati had become the state's CM, but for the first time, she formed a government that was not dependent on anyone's support. For the first time, Mayawati's government was going to run for the state for the entire five years.

Of course, the mobile phone cannot be given complete credit for Mayawati's historic triumph, but it did make the handling of the election much easier. Because of mobile phones, the party's decided narrative could readily reach every village where the party desired to stake its claim to victory.

Jyoti Basu, the then CM of West Bengal and India's doyen of Left politics, was the strongest pillar in making that first mobile call. At the time he received this call, he had been in power in Kolkata for 18 years, and no one saw any threat to him or his party, the Communist Party of India (Marxist) (CPI[M]) or the Left Front led by it for a long time. Jyoti Basu served as CM for another five years until handing over the reins to Buddhadeb Bhattacharya, another party heavyweight. Things changed quickly after that, and Basu's party continued to deteriorate. The Left Front's 34-year-old empire was soon brought down by a party that was only 13 years old—the Mamata Banerjee-led Trinamool Congress (TMC).

Sirpa Tenhunen, an anthropologist from Finland, researched the effects of mobile phones in a West Bengal village in detail.[19] She discovered that mobile phone services played a significant impact in the growth of the TMC. It is ironic how the party whose leader initiated India's first mobile phone call later failed to realize the technology's potential to sway elections. The Left Front was unable to adequately utilize this service and, hence, continued to lag behind.

Tenhunen investigated another effect of mobile phones. She carefully observed the changes brought about by mobile phones

---

[19]Tenhunen, Sirpa, *A Village Goes Mobile: Telephony, Mediation, and Social Change in Rural India*, Oxford University Press, 2018.

in Janta, a village in West Bengal's Bankura district. She focussed her research on a single village at the micro level. She detailed the findings of this study in her book, *A Village Goes Mobile: Telephony, Mediation, and Social Change in Rural India*.

There were only four mobile phones in Janta when Tenhunen arrived in 2003. Two years later, the number went up to 11. Following that, the number rapidly increased, reaching more than 100 in 2007. By 2008, the Dalits of the area had begun to purchase mobile phones.[20]

It was a watershed moment in West Bengal politics. The state government was working on two major projects. One of these was the proposed chemical hub in Nandigram, Purba Medinipur district. [21] The second was Tata's Nano car project at Singur in the Hooghly district. Many organizations in the state, including Mamata Banerjee's TMC, were opposed to both projects. Various rallies and demonstrations were organized in opposition to these plans. During a protest in Nandigram, there was a lot of violence. The Nandigram project was eventually abandoned, and Tata also relocated its Nano project from West Bengal to Gujarat.[22] The politics of the Left front, which began in both these locations, gradually spread to every village.

Tenhunen noted that while politics had begun to change with the introduction of mobile phones, the CPI(M) was still following the same old pattern. She discovered that the party's women's committee was still using letters to organize its meetings in the rural areas. The TMC, on the other hand, began conducting all of this work through mobile phones. The mobile phone had

---

[20]Ibid.

[21]PTI, 'No Chemical Hub at Nandigram: CM', *The Economic Times*, 29 March 2007, http://tinyurl.com/5xx6k86b. Accessed on 13 February 2024.

[22]PTI, 'Tata Motors Ltd Shifted to Gujarat from Singur Because of Law and Order', *The Economic Times*, 22 July 2011, http://tinyurl.com/mvbhe7uy. Accessed on 13 February 2024.

become a channel of communication between the leadership and the grassroots workers for this new party.

From the top down, the CPI(M) had a rigid structure. Any communication used to be delivered from top to bottom, or bottom to top, solely in accordance with an order of command. In the TMC, however, this was not the case. Mamata Banerjee, the party's leader, had a staff of assistants who made and received phone calls on her behalf. Grassroots workers could contact her whenever they wished.[23]

West Bengal's politics is highly complex, and has its own set of issues. Violence at the grassroots level is an essential component of it. Usually, this violence comes from both sides, but many have accused the local police of usually ignoring the Opposition's allegations so they bear the greatest loss. Opposition's activists discovered a weapon to combat it in the form of mobile phones. In the event of any form of violence or excess, they reported it to their senior leaders and received the party's assistance. Small local disputes grew to state and national levels as a result of mobile phones.

In the middle of all of this, Assembly elections were held in West Bengal in 2011. When the election results were announced, the TMC received 184 of the 294 seats in the Assembly. This party was a member of the United Progressive Alliance (UPA), which received 227 seats in that election.[24] The Left Front's 34-year-old fort was entirely demolished. Even after many years, the Left Front has not recovered from this crushing defeat.

The BJP did the same in a much more organized and large-scale setting in 2014, when Amit Shah was running the general election campaign in UP. Anirban Ganguly and Shiwanand Dwivedi's book, *Amit Shah and The March of BJP*, gives us a glimpse of it:

---

[23]Tenhunen, Sirpa, *A Village Goes Mobile: Telephony, Mediation, and Social Change in Rural India*, Oxford University Press, 2018.

[24]Ibid.

> In each assembly segment, groups of workers were formed. Eventually around 4 lakh such dedicated workers were mobilised all over the state to work for the party with a commitment to make it win maximum seats from the state. Each of these workers were also handed out mobile phones and every day the BJP's call centres connected with them through these to keep a tab on the ground realities and the pulse of the voters. Based on their feedback, daily reports were prepared and submitted to Shah who, with his attention for detail and capacity for grasping the intricacies of public sentiment, would identify the problems and the obstacles while sifting through this large amount of data.[25]

Politics was not being altered solely through mobile phone calls. Missed calls from mobile phones soon began to play a major role in politics. BJP issued a number—7505403403—in 2014.[26] Anyone could obtain party membership by making a missed call to this number. When you dialled this number, the call was disconnected, but the number from which you dialled would get preserved in the party's record. Following that, the individual was contacted back for the final part of the membership procedures. A second number, 1800-266-2020, was released shortly after. This time, a few videos were also created for social media, appealing for votes.[27] In one such video, PM Narendra Modi explained the advantages of being a BJP member through mobile phone. Amit Shah, the then-party president, made an appeal to join the BJP in another video.

---

[25]Ganguly, Anirban, and Shiwanand Dwivedi, *Amit Shah and the March of BJP*, Bloomsbury Publishing, 2019.

[26]BJP Uttar Pradesh, *Facebook*, http://tinyurl.com/437xmbcv. Accessed on 13 February 2024.

[27]'#JoinBJP for Empowered India. Give Missed Call on 18002662020 to Become Bjp Member.', YouTube, http://tinyurl.com/3bhhb52n. Accessed on 13 February 2024.

Five years later, as the 2019 elections approached, there was another easy-to-remember missed call membership number: 8980808080. Instead of delegating this task to the organization's regular workers, Cosmic Information and Technology Limited, an Ahmedabad-based IT firm, was hired. Given the enormous number of responses, the party infrastructure would not have been able to handle this campaign.[28]

Following this, it was repeatedly said that 18 crore individuals had joined the party. Every time this figure was mentioned, it was unmistakably stated that the number of BJP members was now greater than the population of many large countries. One advantage of this campaign was that the party had a large database of mobile phone numbers who backed the BJP wholeheartedly.[29] These later had an important influence in politics.

When agitations over the Citizenship (Amendment) Act, 2019 (CAA) and the National Register of Citizens (NRC) erupted across the country in 2020, the BJP took this strategy of missed calls to a new level. Amit Shah, sporting a colourful Rajasthani turban, questioned the audience at a public meeting in Jodhpur. He asked how many from the audience had mobile phones and requested the audience to raise their hands. Additionally, he mentioned that mothers and sisters should also pull out their mobile phones. He then gave a number (8866288662) and repeated it several times. He said that everyone should call this number. He said that missed calls on this number would result in a stern reply to people such as Mamata Banerjee, Arvind Kejriwal and Priyanka Gandhi. He went on to say that their support would reach the PM as a result

---

[28]'BJP Membership Drive',*CIL*, http://tinyurl.com/2mhnb4b6. Accessed on 13 February 2024.

[29]PTI, 'BJP Membership near 18 Crore, Only Seven Countries Have More Population: JP Nadda', *The Times of India*, 29 August 2019, http://tinyurl.com/3wffuuku. Accessed on 13 February 2024.

of this. He then inquired as to who had made a missed call.[30]

Even during non-election periods, mobile phones have become a tool for engaging people and garnering support. It gave BJP followers the impression that they were now directly connected to top leaders. Without a doubt, the BJP obtained useful and credible data from the phone numbers of its followers as a result of this exercise.

The trend that began with the introduction of mobile phones did not end here. By the time West Bengal Assembly elections were held in 2011, next-generation mobile phones or smartphones, had begun to enter the market. The Internet service had also become very popular. And soon the smartphone achieved what even the mobile phone could not.

---

[30]'क्या है Bjp का Miss Call वाला Formula ?' YouTube, http://tinyurl.com/5d2f9urc. Accessed on 13 February 2024.

2

SMARTPHONE: THE NEXT BATTLEGROUND

Any technology becomes smarter over time. There is continuous competition to make it more user-friendly and robust. Especially when it has the potential to be a profitable product in the free market. And that's exactly what happened to mobile phones. They evolved at an unprecedented speed in India.

It is clear that mobile phones have become the fastest-spreading tech in human history.[1] On the other hand, in tandem with the proliferation of mobile phones, the Internet was also advancing rapidly, giving rise to a new set of communication channels such as email and social media. But access to the Internet was very limited in the early days. In order to use it, a computer and a constant source of electrical power were required. And this entire paraphernalia could not be taken anyplace. The world craved a gadget that could surf the web on the go, and that's when the genius of connecting the Internet with mobile phones clicked.

Several mobile phone manufacturers made provisions to connect their phones to the Internet. For example, Blackberry featured numerous features like email and Internet browsing. But their functionality was very limited. The limitations of these mobile phones too were soon left behind. The next stage in the evolution of mobile phones were the smartphones.

---

[1]DeGusta, Michael, 'Are Smart Phones Spreading Faster than Any Technology in Human History?', *MIT Technology Review*, 9 May 2012, http://tinyurl.com/32jb8um9. Accessed on 13 February 2024.

THE AGE OF SMARTPHONES

The smartphone evolved from the mobile phone in many ways, but it was not simply a linear extension of the latter. In many ways, it was diametrically opposed to its predecessor. Smartphones were closer to computers than to mobile phones. The only resemblance was that you could call people and interact via SMS even with a smartphone.

These hand-held devices could perform almost all the functions of a computer. Sometimes, their abilities exceeded a computer's. For example, smartphones with high-resolution cameras could do wonders. These devices even rendered early film cameras redundant. Another strength of the smartphone was that it had been developed in such a way that no training was required to use it. When computers initially arrived in India, coaching institutions were set up in various locations to teach people how to use them. Smartphones, on the other hand, had no such requirement. Anyone could use it with relative ease.

Apple Inc. launched its first iPhone on 9 January 2007.[2] In many ways this was the first smartphone the world had seen. It was the first gizmo that combined the features of multiple standard devices—such as a computer, a camera, a music player and a telephone—into a single, compact unit. Soon after, many more companies entered this sector, thus ushering in the smartphone age.

Soon after, in 2009, the sale of smartphones surpassed that of personal computers (PCs) for the first time in history.[3] The smartphone had emerged as a standard computing platform. It had long been cheaper than computers, but as its market developed

---

[2]'Steve Jobs debuts the iPhone', *History*, 2007, http://tinyurl.com/4saaetnn. Accessed on 13 February 2024.

[3]Weintraub, Seth, 'Industry First: Smartphones Pass PCs in Sales', *Fortune*, 8 February 2011, http://tinyurl.com/vvtveaec. Accessed on 13 February 2024.

rapidly, even cheaper competitors entered the market. It got the ground to reach practically everyone's hands after the debut of Google's Android operating system. Ravi Agarwal's book *India Connected* reveals the role that smartphones played in Indian society. He says:

> In a country with broken infrastructure, it makes life more efficient. It is an escape. In the cramped, tiny homes in which so many live, it is their only privacy. The smartphone will have a profound impact on family life, on all the ways in which Indians live, learn, love, work, and play. Newly connected Indians are already choosing and crafting new destinies. The smartphone offers them a path to a new job and a new economy... In a land that has long judged people by caste and tribe, the smartphone is emerging as a new vehicle for self-definition.[4]

Around 2.5 million smartphones were brought into India within two years, in 2009. This figure grew to 6 million the next year. One year later, in 2011, 1.2 crore smartphones were shipped to India. This figure grew consistently and swiftly. By the time the 2014 general elections rolled around, India had approximately 190 million smartphone users.[5] This gizmo was now ready to make a major political intervention.

FIRST SMARTPHONE ELECTION

The use of smartphones began during the Gujarat Assembly elections in 2012. In this election, it played a crucial role in

---

[4]Agarwal, Ravi, *India Connected: How the Smartphone Is Transforming the World's Largest Democracy*, Oxford University Press, 2018.

[5]'Number of Smartphone Users in India in 2010 to 2023, with Estimates until 2040 (In Millions)', *statista*, http://tinyurl.com/38cwhhfd. Accessed on 13 February 2024.

political communication and strategy. However, this was in the early days of smartphones.

The December 2013 Delhi Assembly elections can be dubbed as the country's first smartphone election. The recently established Aam Aadmi Party (AAP) made remarkable strides with this technology, riding the anti-incumbency wave against the Indian National Congress (INC or the Congress) and aligning with the anti-corruption movement, 'India Against Corruption'. The party most effectively utilized social media to connect with a large audience, and the election results reflected this strategy. Despite initially securing the second position, AAP later went on to form the government. We will discuss how AAP extensively made use of social media in a later chapter. This election established that smartphones now had become an inalienable part of the Indian political landscape. As a result, when the time came for the general elections in 2014, practically all parties began to prioritize the use of smartphones and its ecosystem in their strategy.

Smartphones did not just enable the political parties to reach out to voters very easily, it also had a multifaceted impact on Indian politics. For example, as the smartphones became more popular in India, voter turnout in the general elections increased significantly. In the 2009 elections, approximately 58 per cent of voters voted, whereas the voter turnout in the 2014 general elections was 66.4 per cent—the highest ever poll percentage recorded in a parliamentary election. But this record too did not last long. In 2019, the voter turnout was at 67.1 per cent.[6]

There are multiple possible explanations for this. One explanation could be that the smartphone made the Indian populace more politically aware. Some believe that a huge number of youths, who did not vote earlier, also voted in the 2014 general elections for

---

[6]Jain, Bharti, 'Lok Sabha Elections: At 67.1%, 2019 Turnout's a Record, Election Commission Says', *The Times of India*, 21 May 2019, http://tinyurl.com/yu6bjza2. Accessed on 13 February 2024.

the first time. According to some, smartphones and social media played a significant part in inspiring these young people. There were 2.3 crore voters between the ages of 18 and 19 in the country during the 2014 general elections. Their number rose significantly five years later when the 2019 general elections were held.

BJP TAKES THE LEAD

The BJP made use of this novel technology the most accurately and extensively. Long before the election, the party's prime ministerial candidate, Narendra Modi, created a separate website. The party established a massive IT cell that is still constantly in the spotlight for its actions. To engage with voters and spread the party's message, the BJP established its own WhatsApp groups in practically every town. Units of the party were required at all levels to record films of their programmes, public meetings, protests and so on, and submit them to the district or state headquarters. It was stated that it would be used for the party's archives. However, it was a good method to keep track of what was going on in the organization. This was not conceivable on such a huge scale prior to the smartphone age.

Without any doubt, this strategy proved beneficial for the BJP. When the results were announced, the party had a commanding majority with 282 seats in the Lok Sabha. This was the party's first opportunity to create a government on its own. The BJP's utilization of technology throughout the election campaign was also credited for these outcomes. On the other side, the BJP's rival, the Congress, was technologically falling behind, and it lacked a compelling narrative that a big segment of the population would have accepted. As a result, it suffered a resounding defeat in the elections, and when the results were announced, the Congress had to be content with only 44 seats.

All parties had their own technical experts who knew everything there was to know about using technology. These individuals created specialized smartphone apps for party leaders.

These apps were not intended to be distributed through app stores, and their APK files were installed directly on the smartphone. When the leader arrived in a constituency, he would have the entire knowledge about the area at his fingertips thanks to this app. He would also know the specific local concerns—What are the voters' feelings? Who else is significant in the area? These apps made their job easier.

What happened in this general election was only a prelude to the true role of smartphones in the 2019 general elections. Much had happened in the world of technology, particularly in India, over the span of five years. And the change was so rapid that it had not even been predicted.

The true potential of smartphones lay in the Internet. Connectivity was absolutely crucial for realizing the gadget's true potential. Smartphones were already growing cheaper, but then there was a wave of very cheap made-in-China smartphones. Most people could now afford these smartphones. But this was not enough to address the situation.

India was among the countries with the highest Internet usage rates. Until then, 4G data was available, but its charges were exorbitant. There was no public WiFi anywhere. The AAP made an electoral promise of free WiFi in Delhi, but it does not appear like the promise has been kept. And it wasn't simply an issue specific to Delhi; it was a national one. Typically, people would turn on the data for a short period before turning it off. Due to data restriction, the middle class was experiencing it on a piecemeal basis, but it was the biggest barrier for the lower classes to embrace the world of smartphones. This picture, too, was soon going to change.

THE INTERNET BOOM

Mukesh Ambani, one of the country's richest industrialists, received the licence for mobile Internet and broadband services only a few months after the general election of 2014. Soon after, he announced the introduction of this service under the Jio brand. Although there was a dispute over issuing him a licence, and the matter went to court, this service began on 5 September 2016. Originally, it was said that it would be completely free for three months, but this was then extended to six months. With this short-term freebie offer, a huge portion of the population initially entered the world of smartphones, but the main draw was that the skyrocketing mobile Internet rates were plummeting.[7]

Before that, at one point in 2016, before Jio entered the market, 1 gigabyte (GB) of data in India cost approximately ₹225 rupees. By 2019, Jio drastically slashed it to ₹18.5 per GB.[8] Suddenly, India became the country with the lowest Internet rates. These packages were created so that customers could utilize 2–4 GB of free data per day. Following that, packages with uninterruptible unlimited Internet access appeared.[9]

People had gained access to the entire world via the Internet, and they could connect with it at any moment. This led to the creation of a world where life seemed incomplete without social media and WhatsApp. People were exposed to YouTube in an enormous way for the first time. It quickly became a competitor to traditional television channels and even movies. At the very least, cinema was no longer the monopolistic dominant form of entertainment.

All of this helped Jio become India's largest telecom provider[10]

---

[7]Jadav, Narendra, 'A Review on Reliance Jio Market Entry Strategies and Its Effects on Indian Telecom Industry', *IJCRT*, Vol. 6, No. 1, 2018.

[8]Deck, Andrew, 'How Mukesh Ambani Won India's Mobile Data Price War', *rest of world*, 15 July 2020, http://tinyurl.com/6fn7ctm5. Accessed on 13 February 2024.

[9]'Mobile Data: Why India Has the World's Cheapest', *BBC*, 18 March 2019, http://tinyurl.com/2t3x4z89. Accessed on 13 February 2024.

[10]Singh, Manish, 'How Reliance Jio Platforms Became India's Biggest Telecom Network', *TechCrunch*, 19 June 2020, http://tinyurl.com/5dcxvwmm. Accessed on 13 February 2024.

and the world's third largest[11]. Telecom companies accused Jio of predatory pricing, yet, they too, were forced to decrease rates. The pressure was so intense that Aditya Birla's company, Idea, was forced to merge with Vodafone. In India, the era of low-cost communication services had begun.[12]

The country had 220 million smartphone users[13] in 2015, which rose to 300 million the following year.[14] Jio's service began on a fully commercial basis in 2017, and then onwards this figure has further grown. This was the year when India surpassed the United States (US) as the world leader in mobile data usage.[15] At 7.30 a.m. on 22 December 2017, Amitabh Kant, CEO of NITI Aayog, tweeted: 'Amazing! With 150 cr gigabytes per month of mobile data consumption India is now world's no 1 mobile data consuming country. Its mobile data consumption is higher than USA & China's mobile data consumption put together.'[16]

This was the same year that PM Narendra Modi made a famous comment that is still widely quoted. He stated that the 2019 general

---

[11]Dua, Priyanka, 'How Reliance Jio Became World's Third Largest Telecom Operator?', *GIZBOT*, 10 June 2021, http://tinyurl.com/mperwywx. Accessed on 13 February 2024.

[12]Philipose, Mobis, 'How Reliance Jio Transformed India's Telecom Industry, in Five Charts', *mint*, 16 January 2020, http://tinyurl.com/4vk75ess. Accessed on 13 February 2024.

[13]Pathak, Tarun, 'India Surpasses USA to Become the Second Largest Smartphone Market in the World', *Counterpoint*, 2 February 2016, http://tinyurl.com/mr34mu7z. Accessed on 13 February 2024.

[14]Mukherjee, Writankar, 'India's Smartphone User Base Topped 300 Million in 2016', *The Economic Times*, 24 January 2017, http://tinyurl.com/ydj4cewa. Accessed on 13 February 2024.

[15]Pandey, Navadha, 'India's Data Usage per Smartphone Highest in World at 9.8gb/Month: Report', *mint*, 19 June 2019, http://tinyurl.com/398dr8ny. Accessed on 13 February 2024.

[16]@amitabhk87, X (formerly Twitter), 22 December 2017, 7.30 a.m., http://tinyurl.com/4crscyer. Accessed on 19 February 2024.

elections will be held on smartphones. On 31 March 2017, he addressed party MPs from Jharkhand, Odisha (previously Orissa), Andhra Pradesh, Karnataka and Telangana at his residence at 7, Lok Kalyan Marg (formerly 7 Race Course Road). These were the states where the BJP did not have a government at the time. Prime Minister Modi convened this meeting to determine the approach for general elections in 2019. According to sources, he also stated during the meeting that one should employ technology because it is the means through which today's youth communicate.[17]

That is exactly what transpired. When the time came for the next general election in 2019, India's smartphone subscriptions had surpassed 620 million. If we only consider adults, smartphones had touched more than half the country by then. According to the 2011 census, the number of families in the country was approximately 25 crore.[18] That means that in 2019, each family had more than two smartphone subscriptions on average.[19] In the same year, Ericsson released a telecom sector survey in which it was revealed that India currently had the largest data usage per smartphone.[20]

However, the war in this general election was not conducted solely on smartphones. Rallies, road shows, street meetings, *mohalla* meetings, door-to-door public relations, posters, leaflets and flags all continued to be visible in public. However, the power

---

[17]Pandey, Brijesh, and Anindya Banerjee, '2019 Elections Will Be Fought on Mobile, Says Prime Minister Narendra Modi', *India Today*, 31 March 2017, http://tinyurl.com/3y576nv5. Accessed on 13 February 2024.

[18]'248.8 Million Households Across India; 202 mn Hindus, 31 mn Muslims', *news18.com*, 20 May 2016, http://tinyurl.com/yame5v4k. Accessed on 19 January 2024.

[19]Pherwani, Ashish, 'Playing by New Rules: Media and Entertainment Industry Trends 2020', *Ernst & Young*, 26 March 2021, http://tinyurl.com/tpchytkt. Accessed on 19 February 2024.

[20]'Data Usage per Smartphone Is the Highest in India–Ericsson', *ericsson.com*, 19 June 2019, http://tinyurl.com/36exf4vk. Accessed on 19 February 2024.

of the smartphone has become so closely identified with this election that it has become a theme in and of itself. Everyone wanted to win it through the Google Play Store and the iPhone App Store.

MOBILE APPS

In the build up to the 2019 election, the NaMo (or Narendra Modi app) was the most talked about even though the app was launched much before. It had surpassed 10 million downloads on Android smartphones alone within a few days of its release. The term 'NaMo' was a creative abbreviation of Narendra Modi for the Internet era; its iteration sounded close to the expression used in some Hindu scriptures. The BJP used the NaMo app to reach out to party supporters and voters.[21] According to the claim by the party:

> With just one click, the interactive 'Narendra Modi' app allows the user to connect with the PM. It provides an exclusive and unique opportunity to receive messages and emails directly from the Prime Minister. …it allows users to contribute and earn badges through to-do tasks. One can tune in and listen to the various 'Mann ki Baat' editions of the PM, read his blogs...[22]

In 2019, a video channel, also called NaMo, aired on cable for a few days before disappearing from both the cable network and memory as soon as the elections were completed.[23]

Apart from this, the BJP also had a Bharatiya Janata Party

---

[21]PTI, 'Prime Minister Launches 'Narendra Modi Mobile App'', *The Hindu*, 17 June 2015, http://tinyurl.com/yhzje2hs. Accessed on 13 February 2024.

[22]*Narendramodi.in*, http://tinyurl.com/y39praxx. Accessed on 22 February 2024.

[23]'NaMo TV: It Came, We Saw, It Conquered (The EC). And Now It's Gone.', *The Wire*, 20 May 2019, http://tinyurl.com/4dtcy5xp. Accessed on 13 February 2024.

app[24], which was launched in August 2016.[25] However, due to the party's focus on the NaMo app, this app received less attention. The 2019 general election campaign, like the 2014 one, was centred on PM Modi rather than the BJP. Thus, the party's app had to take a back seat. The Congress, on the other hand, launched an app called Ghar Ghar Congress.[26] It could not generate the same amount of buzz as the NaMo app.[27]

It wasn't just political parties that were developing apps. Some private enterprises and government agencies have launched apps that turn smartphones into tools. With the use of the Election Commission of India's cVIGIL app, one can report instances of model code of conduct violations with photo and video proof. A PWD app was also made available for voters with disabilities. These people could use the Election Commission's assistance to vote using this app.

During this period, a Jalandhar-based startup launched the Neta app. People could use this to rate their MP, MLA, CM and even the PM. Such attempts were likewise only possible in the smartphone era.[28]

WhatsApp was another smartphone app that played a

---

[24]Mathur, Vishal, 'Lok Sabha Elections 2019: Your Smartphone Is Now Your Voting Companion', *News18*, 12 March 2019, http://tinyurl.com/46hevdsz. Accessed on 13 February 2024.

[25]'Bjp Launches Digitalbjp App Connect All Party Members and Office Bearers', *The Indian Express*, 4 August 2016, http://tinyurl.com/5n7fyhfb. Accessed on 13 February 2024.

[26]Mathur, Vishal, 'Lok Sabha Elections 2019: Your Smartphone Is Now Your Voting Companion', *News18*, 12 March 2019, http://tinyurl.com/46hevdsz. Accessed on 13 February 2024.

[27]Khosla Varuni, and Ravi Teja Sharma, 'After AAP, BJP and Congress Launch Smartphone Apps to Woo Urban Middle-Class Voters', *The Economic Times*, 7 June 2014, http://tinyurl.com/yremvmzm. Accessed on 13 February 2024.

[28]'Dive Into India's First Political-Stock Market', *onething.design*, http://tinyurl.com/rpzh36nd. Accessed on 19 February 2024.

significant role in this election. It was a messenger that quickly rose to prominence. Although it was available in the 2014 general elections, it was only in the 2019 general elections that it played a significant role. The amount of fake news circulated through WhatsApp was much higher compared to any other media. As a result, the 2019 general elections have been dubbed as the 'WhatsApp elections'.[29] We will come to that later.

Smartphones quickly began to alter the pomp and tone of conventional rallies. Many times, during PM Modi's public rallies, the crowd flashed their smartphone flashlights almost collectively. This torch began to replace the traditional clapping and chants uttered at rallies, whether it was spontaneous or choreographed. The smartphone had given the election campaign a new optic.

When the results of the seven-phase elections were announced, the BJP had passed the 300-member mark. The party received a record 303 seats, while the Congress received a tiny increase and had to settle for 52 seats.[30] True, the narrative of the election was clearly in favour of the BJP from the start, but the way it used technology to its advantage was clearly visible in the results.

We don't know what the outcome of this general election would have been if there were no smartphones or if Jio hadn't launched the data pricing war. But one thing is certain: without both, this election would have had an entirely different look and feel. Saba Naqvi, a senior journalist, made an important observation following the election results. She wrote in one of her columns: '...technology had changed the playing field—and

---

[29] Arun, Chinmayi, 'India May Be Witnessing the Next 'Whatsapp Election'—And the Stakes Couldn't Be Higher', *The Washington Post*, 25 April 2019, http://tinyurl.com/4u8hk9ff. Accessed on 13 February 2024.

[30] 'Lok Sabha Election Results 2019', *Elections.in*, http://tinyurl.com/bdfusjcm. Accessed on 19 February 2024.

only the BJP knew the new rules of the game. It was, therefore, substantially, and very fully, a post-Jio election.'[31]

However, this was hardly the only instance of smartphone use in politics. Smartphones were only the medium for fake news, conspiracy theories and political hysteria. This occurred all around the world, and much has been written about it. It was social media that played a significant role ensuring that these reached everyone via the smartphone.

Many studies have been conducted, and much has been written on the positive and negative effects that smartphones have had on society. But, for the time being, we will confine ourselves to politics. Writer Pankaj Mishra made an excellent observation regarding the shift in society's thinking caused by smartphones, which is affecting many things, including politics: 'Smartphone owners are constantly exposed to high volumes of information and disinformation—both of which have a misleadingly uniform digital texture. One obvious result is the weakening of analytic ability—the capacity to distinguish between the essential and the inessential, truth and untruth.'[32]

If the election campaign is a battleground, the smartphone has become its most powerful weapon. As a medium of communication, it brings politics into every home and allows every citizen to participate in the electoral discourse based on their grasp of thinking. It also broadcasts the electoral narrative and keeps adding new chapters to it continuously.

---

[31]Naqvi, Saba, 'Mobile Politics: Why I Think Lok Sabha 2019 Was Not a Post-mandal but a Post-jio Election', *dailyo.in*, 19 June 2019, http://tinyurl.com/mvdcf6h5. Accessed on 19 February 2024.

[32]Mishra, Pankaj, 'View: Future of Democracy Is Literally in India's Hands', *The Economic Times*, 21 April 2019, http://tinyurl.com/4xcfmjd5. Accessed on 22 February 2024.

3

ORWELLIAN DATABASE OF VOTERS' RECORDS

The Influence Industry Project[1] is an organization that studies how data and technology can be used to influence politics. Data is beneficial for political parties in three ways, according to the classification done by this organization.

1. **Data as an asset**: Data acquired in various ways and from diverse sources is used to develop a thorough profile of each voter. Where he lives, what he does for a living, what he reads, what websites he visits, where and how he is active on social media, his caste, religion and all other information are stored with his name, address and other contact information.
2. **Data as intelligence**: The process of analysing the data acquired in this manner is crucial. This information is then utilized to develop predictions about each voter. What is his ideology? What are his political beliefs? And, in the end, which party or candidate will his vote go to? This also indicates who among this group of voters can donate to the party's fundraising efforts.
3. **Data as political influence**: It is then decided how to reach these voters, influence them and keep them engaged

[1] *The Influence Industry Project*, http://tinyurl.com/mr2b3b9t. Accessed on 22 February 2024.

indefinitely. This also determines what type of message is sent to which voter. Big data is the window through which you can understand your voter while also entirely changing his experience of connecting with the political narrative. If you totally grasp your voter and make them feel connected to your narrative, you have already won more than half the battle.

WHAT IS BIG DATA?

The Internet has become an inseparable part of our lives. From grocery shopping, finding the fastest route to our destination to mobile banking, we regularly access information and have become overly reliant on the Internet.

When we use online services, they collect our information to make our experience better. This creates a lot of data every day, and this can loosely be called Big Data. When you're on the Internet, your data is gathered in different ways. Websites use cookies (small files on your device) to remember what you do and like. Web analytics tools watch how you use websites, and social media sites learn from what you post and engage with. For example, if you enjoy short clips from Shah Rukh Khan movies on a social platform, you'll notice that suggested videos are often from movies featuring the same actor. Another instance is how search engines remember what you search for and where you go online. If you look for a book, you might see ads from an online store selling the same book following you online for a few days.

The sheer volume of information gathered on individuals is extensive, personal and revealing. They capture our conversations, expressions and content consumption, including images, movies, music and news. There are even claims[2] that data analytics can

---

[2]Kuhn, George, 'How Target Used Data Analytics to Predict Pregnancies', 1 August 2023, http://tinyurl.com/bdv3tp4n. Accessed on 22 February 2024.

predict a woman's pregnancy and anticipated delivery date solely by analysing her Instagram posts. They accomplish this by gathering large amounts of data, analysing patterns and employing prediction models to identify potential life events, such as pregnancy, allowing businesses to tailor their marketing efforts to specific client segments. It seems that almost every aspect of our lives is on track to be documented.

In their report, *Data and Democracy in the Digital Age*, Stephanie Hankey, Julianne Kerr Morrison and Ravi Naik give us clarity on the same:

> In particular, individual opinions and behaviour can be cross-correlated with that of thousands of similar people, achieving an uncanny understanding of individual personality sets. These profiles are probably more predictive than what the individual could achieve through introspection (for instance, it has been suggested that Facebook 'likes' enable algorithms to assess your personality better that your own friends could). As recent political scandals have shown, they can predict which side you will ultimately vote for in an election. And it's not just individual-level profiling power—large groups can be even more predictable, as aggregating data points erases randomness and individual outliers.[3]

There are various avenues available to create profiles of voters; all that is needed is data. In India, there are two types of basic data freely available for politics. The first is the electoral roll, popularly known as the voters' list. The second is the complete results of the several elections. By the way, both of these have existed since before modern data analytics, but data analytics has altered their meaning through value addition.

---

[3]Hankey, Stephanie, Julianne Kerr Morrison and Ravi Naik, *Data and Democracy in the Digital Age*, The Constitution Society, 10 July 2018, http://tinyurl.com/48szwmkm. Accessed on 19 February 2024.

TURNING THE VOTER LIST INTO BIG DATA

The voters' list data is massive, but it cannot be called Big Data. The latter is not only vast in size, but it also grows all the time, continuously and rapidly. In the 2019 general elections, there were 912 million registered voters in the country.[4] In contrast, a voters' list is a static data set whose size does not grow automatically. To use the voters' list data, it needs to be turned into Big Data. There are multiple ways political parties turn the voters' list data into Big Data in order to devise effective polling strategies. One approach to accomplish this is to add people's phone numbers and social media IDs to the voters' list database, which opens up several opportunities for constant engagement with them as well as helps add all of their activities to the database.

Obtaining phone numbers of people can be tough in the rest of the world, but it is not so difficult in India. People easily give their phone number and often their email address as well. There are numerous approaches to this. To begin, the mobile apps of the parties are a major source of this. The party receives the phone numbers and other information of users who installed the app. That's not all. Consider the NaMo app. When you install it, it asks for permission to access your location, contacts, photographs, camera and microphone. All such information is freely available to the server that runs the app.

There are numerous more methods available. For example, a political party may organize a yoga camp through one of its non-political affiliates. It is not at all odd or unusual to ask the participants there to share their names, addresses and phone numbers. A simple social service event where participants are looking forward to better health can actually just be a data collection exercise. People there will undoubtedly learn some vital yoga asanas, but what the political party gains from it will

---

[4]Statistical Report of General Election 2019, by Election Commission of India.

be far more useful. Next, let us see how these phone numbers are used to woo the voters.

A perfect example for using collected numbers is what happened in Ghaziabad district in UP, when local body elections were held in the first half of 2023. Vasundhara and Indirapuram are two colonies in the Ghaziabad district's Trans Hindon area. The metro service in Delhi has reached neighbouring colonies but not there. This was also planned multiple times but never came to fruition.

In these colonies, the main complaint was that the metro does not reach them. Many such WhatsApp groups began to form there six months before the local body elections, one after the other: Metro Sangharsh Morcha, Metro Vistar Samiti and so on. For a long time, there was just chatter about metro service. When the elections arrived, the election campaign began in the WhatsApp groups. Following the elections, these groups almost ceased to exist. However, by that time, numerous numbers from a certain area had entered a party's database.[5]

GEOFENCING

When you arrive at an airport and turn on your phone, you are likely to get a message asking you to dial a particular number for a taxi. Just as you approach a clothing store in the vicinity, you unexpectedly receive a message prompting you to explore another fashion outlet with a fantastic offer. The curiosity arises about how they obtained your phone number and how they are aware of your current location. Geofencing technology is employed in such communication.

Geofencing creates a type of a digital fence. The message can be sent in such a way that only those inside the fence will receive it, while those outside will not. The message will not only reach the

[5]From the author's own field reporting.

folks, but their phone numbers will reach the database as well. In an interview with *Business World*, marketing guru Aseem Mangal confirmed that geofencing is used to gather mobile numbers.[6]

It is utilized right within the polling station when voting in countries such as US. People in queue for voting are given one final message about who they should vote for. Phones are normally not permitted inside polling stations in India, therefore such a use is unlikely here. However, it can be utilized for data collection.

The BJP has chosen a more dependable method of gathering such ground data. When Amit Shah was national president, the party created posts for a number of '*panna pramukhs*' for each polling booth. Panna pramukh refers to the person in charge of each page of the electoral roll.[7] One page of the voters list usually has information of 60 voters on both sides of the page. The panna pramukh must first determine who among these are likely to vote for the party, who will not vote for the party and who can be persuaded to vote for the party. He also forms WhatsApp groups of these individuals, and all of this information eventually strengthens the party's database. There is no finer example of grassroots political data collection at the neighbourhood level. On election day, it is the page in charge's responsibility to ensure that all the party supporters on his page visit the polling station and vote.

WHAT'S THE ENDGAME?

We saw in the first chapter how the BJP used audio messages from Atal Bihari Vajpayee to make phone calls during the 2004

---

[6]'Aseem Mangal On How To Create A Digital Strategy For Political Campaign', *businessworld.in*, 18 November 2021, http://tinyurl.com/2ctdhshx. Access on 19 February 2024.

[7]Ganguly, Anirban, and Shivanand Dwivedi, *Amit Shah and the March of BJP*, Bloomsbury, 2019, p. 140.

general elections. It was just a publicity stunt at the time. It is still a prevalent tactic, but it is also significant in Big Data mining. It may be the case that now when political parties make these calls, the time when the caller disconnects is recorded. And this data can be read in many ways. Did he hear all they said? Or did he disconnect after only half listening? Or did he cut the call before the first sentence was finished? This can be used to generate a variety of profiles: individuals who support the party and its leader; people who are kind to them; or individuals who simply despise them.

Big Data can significantly influence voters' experiences with political affiliations. Political parties use data gathered from social media platforms to tailor their messages. For instance, on YouTube, you can decide if your ad should reach those watching Congress or BJP videos. On Google, you have the option to choose the type of search result where your ad appears. According to Shivam Shankar Singh, Facebook's internal data indicates how closely the company observes politicians' use of its platform. Facebook is designed for this type of advertising, allowing ads to be tested and targeted at specific groups based on their likes, interests and demographics. The same principle applies to other social media platforms as well.[8]

Another application of data involves assessing the popularity of local MLAs or MPs. In the past, this process required surveys and other methods, but today it can be swiftly conducted on a large scale. Lengthy field surveys are no longer necessary; conducting a few phone calls with an appropriate sample size allows you to gauge the ground situation within hours. In previous elections, it was observed that the BJP refrained from giving tickets to several of its incumbent MLAs and MPs, benefitting from this

---

[8]Singh, Shivam Shankar, *How to Win an Indian Election*, Penguin Random House, 2019.

strategic move.[9] Big data not only aids in formulating strategies to secure the maximum votes but also serves to address and rectify the party's weaknesses.

We mentioned another type of basic data at the beginning of this chapter. That is the election results data. Its application is restricted but crucial in the context of elections. Typically, election results up to the booth level are provided. It shows where and who received how many votes. This is critical for political parties, as it shows them where they are strong, where they are weak, where they need to work harder and where they need to make some arrangements with another party. Parties consider the outcomes of the previous election while developing their electoral strategy. Its macro analysis indicates the resources required by the party.

When compared to traditional election campaigns, data-driven election campaigns completely altered the rules of the game. Some commentators divide election campaigns into two eras: Before Big Data (BBD) and After Big Data (ABD).[10] Traditional election campaigns required a huge number of workers at the grassroots level to undertake door-to-door public relations, paste posters, host street meetings or hold large rallies. These workers were regarded as the backbone of any political campaign. However, professionals, not workers, are required for a data-driven electoral campaign. Traditional politics required a huge number of workers to transmit the word to the public. However, in today's world, just a few professionals are needed to do so. This demand for expertise has provided opportunities for businesses to participate in the election campaign. This aspect will be covered in depth in the third part of this book.

---

[9]Mishra, Abhinandan, 'BJP to Deny Tickets to 125 MPs, Hopes to Gain Pro-incumbency Momentum', *sundayguardianlive.com*, 31 December 2023, http://tinyurl.com/4t438ncc. Accessed on 19 February 2024.

[10]Lucas, Anthony, 'Recognizing the "Big Data" Problem', *datafloq.com*, 15 January 2020, http://tinyurl.com/yhacdvkc. Accessed on 19 February 2024.

EVER-INCREASING POLARIZATION IN SOCIETY

Big Data-driven political campaigns have intensified societal polarization by leveraging vast amounts of personal information to tailor messages and target specific demographics. Many experts have pointed out that as a result of this, not only is societal polarization continuously increasing, but it is also becoming more pronounced. Chuck Todd and Carrie Dann have demonstrated in an NBC programme how polarization in society has intensified since the emergence of Big Data by using election data from the US.[11] There were once two poles of voters. And there were a considerable number of voters between these two, whom we referred to as 'fence sitters' or 'persuadable voters'. According to this analysis, the percentage of such persuadable voters in the US is steadily declining, and the majority of voters are on either end of the pole. This divide occurs well before the voting.

We don't need to travel to the US to comprehend this, it's occurring right here in India. This polarization is much more obvious in state legislature elections. We can take the most recent Assembly elections in West Bengal as an example. The entire political landscape became polarized between the TMC and the BJP. The CPI (M) and the Congress, which dominated West Bengal for years, were nearly wiped out in this election. Until recently, Mayawati's BSP was a prominent political force in UP. The previous state election, however, was so polarized between the BJP and the Samajwadi Party that the BSP was completely marginalized.

The polarization of politics that we have witnessed in recent years is not limited to election season. Its fire appears to flare up a little more during elections, but it never goes out. In many ways,

---

[11]Todd, Chuck, and Carrie Dann, 'How Big Data Broke American Politics', *NBC News*, 15 March 2017, http://tinyurl.com/2kney6ua. Accessed on 19 February 2024.

it has also divided society into two halves. Efforts to maintain this polarization are also ongoing. This is why all of the country's major leaders are always seen campaigning. Even when there is no election around, they continue to discuss in order to establish polarization. This form of polarization is seen not only in India, but also in the US, the United Kingdom and many other countries.

Aggression has increased in society as a result of this polarization. This aggressiveness has also given rise to a variety of forms of hatred. One of the most apparent instances is what happened on Capitol Hill after Donald Trump was defeated in the US election. Many examples can be found virtually every other day in our country as well. This polarization has not only created the conditions for things like fake news, but it has also given many people the mindset wherein they are willing to trust everything blindly.

POSSIBLE DATA LEAK

It has also been observed that the ruling party easily possesses a wide range of public data. A case from Andhra Pradesh sparked great debate a few years ago. It was claimed that the Telugu Desam Party gave a large amount of data about government scheme recipients to a company called IT Grid. It was also claimed that as a result of this, information on unique identification numbers (UIDs) had reached this company. However, the organization in charge of the UID system dismissed any such concerns.[12]

Similarly, we learn about acquiring voters' data for political objectives from a *Hindustan Times* report. This report is on the BJP's election campaign in 2019. Jervis Technology and Strategy Consulting Private Limited was one of the professional firms

[12]Lasania, Yusuf Y., 'TDP Faces Heat Over Probe Into It Firm for Data Theft', *mint*, 5 March 2019, http://tinyurl.com/5v6a6dzy. Accessed on 19 February 2024.

that assisted the BJP in this election.[13] According to the report, the beneficiaries of the central government's initiatives such as 'Ujjwala' and 'Swachh Bharat' were the first to be targeted for the elections. People were provided free cooking gas under the Ujjwala scheme, and toilets were built in their homes under Swachh Bharat. Although this article did not precisely explain how they obtained such data, if someone is obtaining data of government scheme beneficiaries, it is a case of data leak at some level.

Shivam Shankar Singh—author of *How to Win an Indian Election* who has also worked with Indian Political Action Committee (I-PAC) in Punjab and the BJP in the Northeast—shares his experience of collecting a different type of data.[14] He argues that the best approach to determine a family's economic status is to obtain their electricity bill. He claims that power supply firms are now paying attention to data security, which was not previously the case. If you want, you could download the electricity bills of all the users in a given area from the power company's website. In fact, there are many more methods of gathering personal information than we have shown here. It is easier in India because there are neither rigorous data privacy regulations nor widespread awareness of the issue.

When the Cambridge Analytica scandal broke in 2018, both Cambridge Analytica and Facebook stood in the dock, and the world realized the danger of this business.

The scandal[15] shows how this data can be utilized politically. Cambridge Analytica was the British firm in charge of the election campaign. This startup had released an app called 'This Is Your

---

[13]Dutta, Anisha, 'How BJP Used Data to Craft Landslide Win', *Hindustan Times*, 25 May 2019, http://tinyurl.com/2cfc4sfm. Accessed on 13 February 2024.

[14]Personal interview

[15]Kaiser, Brittany, *Targeted: The Cambridge Analytica Whistleblower's inside Story of How Big Data, Trump, and Facebook Broke Democracy and How It Can Happen Again*, HarperCollins, 2019.

Digital Life'. A deceptive name that suggests the software is for anything like privacy protection. However, the contrary was true. It acquired not only users' Facebook data but also the data of their Facebook friends. Using this information, psychological profiles of people were created, and personalized campaign messages were distributed to everyone. This firm handled political campaigns in a variety of nations, the most notable of which was the 2016 US presidential election, in which this firm devised and implemented Donald Trump's election strategy.

When a whistleblower revealed the issue in 2018, it was discovered that Facebook was fully aware of it and allowed it to occur. Following the uproar surrounding Cambridge Analytica, Facebook vowed to develop such a mechanism so that no third party could harvest its users' data in this manner. However, this practice cannot be considered to have ended entirely. In any case, we only know about Facebook from this matter; we don't know if or not data from other social media platforms were used in this manner. There have also been allegations that social media platforms attempted to mould public opinion in favour of one candidate during election season.[16]

It is also vital to emphasize that Cambridge Analytica has been doing business in India. It worked for a number of candidates and political parties. When this became public, both the BJP and the Congress levelled accusations at one other. An investigation was also launched. However, the findings of this investigation were not made available.

Numerous companies, digital startups, data brokers and data agents sell large amounts of phone numbers, email addresses and social network IDs for a price. Builders, financing firms, telemarketing companies and even scammers are among their

[16]Fujiwara, Thomas, Karsten Muller and Carlo Schwarz, 'The Effect of Social Media on Elections: Evidence from the United States', *Princeton.edu*, 2023, http://tinyurl.com/3pzmxx5e. Accessed on 13 February 2024.

regular clients.[17] There is no reason to suppose that political parties or companies involved in propaganda would not purchase data from them. In the US, Aristotle Inc., a company infamous for mining voter data for political campaigns, has been an essential campaign tool for every president since Ronald Reagan. Their database has grown so enormous and crucial to the overall plan that it has been dubbed as the 'Orwellian Database of Voters' Records'.[18]

---

[17]Sarkhel, Aritra, 'How Data Brokers Are Selling All Your Personal Info for Less than a Rupee to Whoever Wants It', *The Wire*, 28 February 2017, http://tinyurl.com/3wwh9x5v. Accessed on 13 February 2024.

[18]Verini, James, 'Big Brother Inc.', *VanityFair*, 12 December 2007, http://tinyurl.com/bddv2a6d. Accessed on 13 February 2024.

PART TWO

INFLUENCERS

4

SOCIAL MEDIA: THE NARRATIVE BUILDER

Within the first two decades of the twenty-first century, social media has ushered in an irreversible transformation in global politics. One key and profound change it has initiated is the heightened involvement of the youth in politics. It has provided young individuals living under autocratic governments with a novel means to express themselves and come together. In December 2010, Tunisia's youth utilized social media to mobilize against the government, taking their protest to the streets. This movement persisted for several months and spread across various West Asian countries. Consequently, governmental changes occurred in certain regions, while in others these uprisings were quelled.

INDIA AGAINST CORRUPTION

Soon, India, too, witnessed a surge of protests that profoundly altered the destiny of the nation. The catalyst for these demonstrations was the revelation of multiple scandals, such as the 2G, Coalgate and Commonwealth Games controversies involving ministers of the UPA-II administration under PM Manmohan Singh.

Unfolding in 2011, the India Against Corruption (IAC) movement materialized as a series of protests nationwide, specifically targeting political corruption. The movement, led by social activist Anna Hazare, gained momentum in response to the government's reluctance to heed the growing demands for the establishment of a national anti-corruption body (the Lok Pal) endowed with the authority to investigate political corruption.

The IAC movement made its presence felt by harnessing the power of social media. Within months of the movement being launched in April 2011, it roped in lakhs of followers on Facebook. The movement drew a whole lot of bright young Indians including IT professionals who left their high-end lucrative jobs. The appeal of the movement made it a social media sensation. Apart from the official page, more than 150 Facebook pages associated with 'Anna Hazare' and 'India Against Corruption' surfaced. Interestingly, the majority of these pages appear to have been created by various enthusiasts who were not officially affiliated with Anna's team.[1]

Eventually, the success of this movement led to the formation of the AAP. On 26 November 2012, the AAP was officially announced.[2] The AAP's leaders, who were once Hazare's close associates, were determined to exploit social media for the success of the party, after witnessing firsthand what social media did for the IAC movement.

The AAP was very likely the first party in the country whose formation was streamed live on YouTube.[3] There was a lot of activity on social media as soon as the party was created. Fifteen workers were tasked with developing 800 Facebook pages for each state.[4] The party received the majority of its donations via social media. It had 220 volunteers trained for social media. According to later reports, the party had a total of 10,151 campaigners who were

---

[1]Ohri, Kapil, 'How Powerful Is Anna Hazare on Facebook and Twitter?', *afaqs!*, 18 August 2011, http://tinyurl.com/bdcvvwne. Accessed on 15 February 2024.

[2]Lal, Ankit, *India Social: How Social Media Is Leading the Charge and Changing the Country* , Hachette India, 2017.

[3]Ibid. 38.

[4]Ibid. 38.

constantly reaching out to 3,515,135 people.[5] Several times, the party had live debates via Twitter (now X) chat. This conversation could begin at any time, and a significant number of people would quickly join in. Social media monitoring corporations, commonly known as social listening firms, reported for months prior to the election that Arvind Kejriwal had gained an edge in Delhi.[6]

Kejriwal was the first one to translate social media support into votes. Whenever the AAP is mentioned, two things immediately come to mind: (i) Arvind Kejriwal and (ii) the usage of social media. Some even claim that the AAP and Arvind Kejriwal only have clout owing to social media. Aside from that, Arvind Kejriwal had 1.5 million Twitter followers in 2011, which climbed to 3.6 million in the following two years.

While it is true that AAP launched several campaigns solely on social media in the beginning, it also steadily reinforced itself at the grassroots. They demonstrated this by establishing the government not once, but three times. For the party, social media was a means to an end, not an end in itself. This is how the party has persisted for so long. 'I think technology has been our saviour,' says AAP leader Somu Sundaram. 'Without social media, we would not have been able to contact as many people.'[7]

NIRBHAYA

Social media again became a clotting factor in the next wave of protests after the IAC movement. This time too, the youth played the most important role. On 16 December 2012, a 23-year-old

---

[5]Dhapola, Shruti, 'Delhi Polls: Aap Leads on Twitter, Facebook, but Is It Enough?', *Firstpost.*, 3 December 2013, http://tinyurl.com/y2p4tubr. Accessed on 15 February 2024.

[6]Ibid.

[7]'Truth vs Hype: Trending #Democracy', *NDTV Elections*, 8 December 2013, http://tinyurl.com/44j8dfj8. Accessed on 15 February 2024.

girl was raped in a moving bus in South Delhi by a group of men. They brutalized her body before abandoning her on the side of the road. To conceal the girl's identity, the media gave her the moniker 'Nirbhaya', and this case became known as the 'Nirbhaya incident'.

Those were tough times for Delhi. Anger could be seen and felt on every face and every street throughout the city. Four days after the incident, a group of young people gathered near India Gate for a candlelight protest. They held signs that read 'We want justice'.[8] Such protests had occurred previously, but this protest was not restricted to a candlelight vigil. Within a few hours, a sizeable number of young people started gathering there, and the crowd continued to grow. The next day, these young people made their way to the road between North and South Blocks, towards the Rashtrapati Bhavan.

December is a very cold month in Delhi, and despite the temperature these young people remained there around the clock. The police and the administration were confused about what to do. All of the nearby metro stations were shut down. Police used barricades to block several roads. But it made no difference. On 22 December, the cops also attempted to be a little stricter. Water cannons were used, tear gas shells were fired and a moderate lathi charge was carried out. However, it had little effect.[9]

These were the same cops who had dealt with far larger and more aggressive political demonstrations in the past. Protesters were never before allowed to walk the area where all of this uproar was taking place. Nevertheless, considering that the gathering mostly consisted of middle-class youth, the cops seemed incapable

---

[8]Bhandare, Namita, 'What Women Want', *mint*, 8 March 2014, http://tinyurl.com/2h84kjf8. Accessed on 15 February 2024.

[9]PTI, 'Delhi Gang Rape Case: Teargas, Water Cannons Used against Protesters', *The Times of India*, 22 December 2012, http://tinyurl.com/ymzczcz8. Accessed on 15 February 2024.

of taking any big action against them.The administration also ordered them to exercise restraint, as they were well aware that even a small amount of strictness could jeopardize its reputation.

The political parties often dismissed these young people as having little interest in politics as long as their careers and lifestyle remained unaffected. The sheer number of such young people at this spontaneous gathering on Rajpath surprised everyone, notably the political parties. There were at least 10 groups that were created on Facebook overnight, urging people to go to Rajpath and join the demonstration.[10] Many of the youth political organizations' members had already engaged in these demonstrations before their organizations could understand anything.

Social media was buzzing with calls for a change from ordinary citizens and prominent figures alike. Shruti Upadhyay, a student at the Centre for Social Work in Mumbai, organized a protest at Juhu to collect signatures for a petition demanding capital punishment for the six alleged rapists. The event, 'Enough is Enough', was organized through Facebook.[11] During this time, Bangladeshi author Taslima Nasreen tweeted: 'Women get raped in India every 20 min. But the authority doesn't want women to protest against rape. Not even for 20 min. #DelhiGangRape.'[12] In a very short span of time it received 200 retweets. Several hashtags associated with this trended on Twitter.[13]

All of this was not limited to Delhi. Similar youth demonstrations started surfacing from Bangalore (now Bengaluru),

---

[10]Prasad, Akanksha, and Indu Nandakumar, 'Delhi Gang Rape Case: Social Media Fuels Rally at India Gate', *The Economic Times*, 24 December 2012, http://tinyurl.com/4z5dm8sh. Accessed on 15 February 2024.

[11]Ibid.

[12]@taslimanasreen, X (formerly Twitter), 22 December 2012, 12.47 p.m., http://tinyurl.com/yxkmjw4s. Accessed on 19 February 2024.

[13]Prasad, Akanksha, and Indu Nandakumar, 'Delhi Gang Rape Case: Social Media Fuels Rally at India Gate', *The Economic Times*, 24 December 2012, http://tinyurl.com/4z5dm8sh. Accessed on 15 February 2024.

Lucknow, Patna, Bhopal, Kolkata, Guwahati and nearly every other part of the country.

Outside of social media, this uprising could be found all over the Internet. The top search phrases during that time period were 'Delhi gang rape', 'Rape in Delhi' and 'Gang rape victim', according to a Google Trend search.[14]

There were numerous parallels drawn between the Delhi protests and the Arab Spring. Social media had a significant influence in both cases. The Arab Spring was dubbed the hashtag revolution, and the same phrase was applied to Indian protests following the Nirbhaya incident. When the uprising began in Tunisia, the ever-connected smartphone was already in the hands of the masses and social media was in their grasp. Similar things can be said about the 2012 protest on Delhi's Rajpath. By that time, 4G service was available and protestors could reach out to the rest of the youth via social media. The Arab Spring's largest and most publicized demonstration took place at Cairo's Tahrir Square. A protest on Rajpath in New Delhi was also witnessed in conjunction with this. When actor and film director Shekhar Kapur tweeted about the comparison ('Delhi looks more like India's Tahrir Square'[15]) it quickly received over 100 retweets.

Looking back, there is an obvious distinction between the Arab Spring demonstrations and the protests following the Nirbhaya incident. During the Arab Spring, the youth spoke out against the dictatorship. They were challenging the entire system. It was a more difficult and riskier task. They were demonstrating in a region where such protests were prohibited. Their problem was that the rule of many countries had become more autocratic and repressive. The system they wanted to get from their movement already existed in India. This is why the movement that began in

---

[14]Ibid.

[15]@shekharkapur, X (formerly Twitter), 22 December 2012, 11.42 a.m., http://tinyurl.com/3j2zramx. Accessed on 19 February 2024.

India has at least succeeded in changing the law. There may have been various things mentioned about a number of movements around the country and the people affiliated with them, but there was never any report of suppression of the people associated with the Rajpath agitation, other than sporadic minor lathi charges and the use of tear gas shells.

This was India's first significant political showdown on social media. This also demonstrated the political significance of social media to those political parties who had previously avoided it. Them joining the social media bandwagon gave the parties a new tool to connect with the public.Then, numerous such studies[16] were published, revealing that the young generation's primary source of news is now the social media rather than traditional media.

NARENDRA MODI SHOWS THE WAY

Leaders are supposed to win elections not by the issues they raise, but by the stories they tell. People generally do not identify with political problems, political parties or politicians; they most easily engage with political narratives, in which stories play an important role. You may not only produce stories on social media, you can also use them as a torrential shower, bring the floods with it and even generate tsunamis of stories. In the politics of elections, what kind of stories and how they are used to touch people's hearts has an effect. There is a significant distinction between traditional and social media politics. Traditional politics is more of a one-way path to disseminate propaganda, whereas social media politics enables you to engage people. Politicians quickly learnt how to do this. And Narendra Modi took the lead.

---

[16]Galan, Lucas, et al., *How Young People Consume News and the Implications for Mainstream Media*, Flamingo (Commissioned by Reuters Institute for the Study of Journalism, Oxford University), http://tinyurl.com/4eea9scy. Accessed on 15 February 2024.

When he was the CM of Gujarat, he recognized the significance of social media and fully embraced it. He joined Twitter in 2009[17] and afterwards joined Facebook[18], along with starting his blog[19]. He soon after started his own website. This website was out was out-and-out social media friendly. Without any effort, each sentence of it could be tweeted separately.

According to an *Indian Express* report from 2012, then CM Narendra Modi began to develop a vast social media network on a large scale across the country. It was under the leadership of his Officer on Special Duty (OSD), Hiren Joshi, in Ahmedabad that a team of 2,000 people were tasked with tweeting for Modi, posting in his support on social media and creating blogs, among other things. In the middle of these attempts, the BJP established an IT unit with such a large network that how many individuals work there is still unknown. The BJP's IT cell has established the standards for how and to what degree social media can be used in politics.[20]

Modi's rallies were aired live on YouTube and Facebook from the very beginning. Although most of his rallies were full, there were numerous gatherings where more people were following him on social media than listening to him on the ground. People's reliance on traditional media had begun to dwindle as a result of social media. This was the era when the term 'live webcasting' became popular. This was also vital, since

---

[17]Rampal, Nikhil, 'From CM to PM, How Narendra Modi's Twitter Content Changed in 10 Years', *India Today*, 7 May 2019, http://tinyurl.com/s2b3yer8. Accessed on 15 February 2024.

[18]'CM Receives 1 Million Fans on Facebook', *Narendra Modi*, 6 November 2012, http://tinyurl.com/kcz3z8d6. Accessed on 15 February 2024.

[19]His blogs are available on the website, *Narendra Modi*, https://www.narendramodi.in/blog. Accessed on 15 February 2024; He wrote his first blog on 10 January 2010.

[20]'The Men behind Narendra Modi', *The Indian Express*, 10 June 2013, http://tinyurl.com/yc6ux25u. Accessed on 15 February 2024.

Narendra Modi was not only connecting with Indian nationals, but also with those who are known as Non-Resident Indians (NRIs). He continues to use the Indian diaspora around the world as his political capital.

When there are political rallies or party programmes, suitable arrangements are usually established so that media reporters can file their reports quickly and efficiently. Computer systems are installed nearby, and WiFi is set up for email. Arrangements for typewriters, telegrams and fax machines, among other things, were made prior to the event. During a Narendra Modi event, held in Mumbai's Bandra Kurla Complex in December 2013, arrangements were made for journalists as well as social media professionals to easily tweet, post on Facebook and update their blogs.[21] Social media had finally caught up to traditional media!

Modi found novel ways to make use of social media. In March 2014, he launched a mobile application, India272+. The India272+ app allowed users to participate in discussions and debates, sharing ideas for the then Gujarat CM's speeches. The app made it convenient for volunteers to connect with other volunteers. It also enabled them to share pictures, clippings of popular news stories and blogs. Popular social media platforms like Facebook, Twitter, WhatsApp were integrated in the app, making it possible for the users to share updates through social media.[22]

Modi's social media team did two things together. First, they regularly worked to make him look good, pushing a larger-than-life image of Modi in the minds of the voters. Second, in doing so, they launched a digital assault on the Congress.

---

[21]Chopra, Shaili, *The Big Connect: Politics in the Age of Social Media*, Random House Publishers, 2014.

[22]'Narendra Modi Launches Mobile App for INDIA272+', *India Today*, 26 March 2014, http://tinyurl.com/su5dserf. Accessed on 15 February 2024.

Hailing Modi's economic policies, the term 'Gujarat Model' was launched. At the same time, then PM Manmohan Singh was dubbed 'Maun Mohan Singh', or 'the man who doesn't open his lips'.[23] His administration was accused of suffering from a policy paralysis. The 'Grand Old Party' was already on a backfoot with an array of corruption allegations levelled against its prominent faces. BJP's social media team successfully built a narrative on social media that the 'Gujarat Model' and Modi were the country's sole viable choice.

HOW CONGRESS LOST

Unlike BJP's proactive approach to social media, the Congress decided to stay out of it. In many respects, the Congress may be credited with launching the IT revolution in India, but the party's reluctance to embrace its outcomes was puzzling. Former PM Manmohan Singh had emphatically refused to make a social media account. For a long time, Rahul Gandhi, the youngest of the senior Congress leaders, ignored Twitter's strength and necessity. Some of Rahul's close associates, often referred to as 'Team Rahul', also showed no interest in being active on social media. Shashi Tharoor was the sole member of Congress who used Twitter. In some ways, he was India's first social media celebrity. He was most likely the first politician in India to master the art of making headlines and controversies over Twitter. However, he was unable to persuade the party to establish an online presence.

Using social media as a weapon, the BJP and AAP were continually assaulting PM Manmohan Singh, all of his ministers, Sonia Gandhi and Rahul Gandhi. At the time, a massive narrative was being crafted against the Congress. This could only be

---

[23]"In Himachal,Modi Mocks PM,Calls Him "Maun Mohan"", *The Indian Express*, 30 October 2012, http://tinyurl.com/bdfpa9yv. Accessed on 15 February 2024.

responded to on social media. However, there was little planning and there was no passion for it within the Congress. There was also no overarching strategy necessary on how to be engaging on social media.

Initially, Congress's participation in social media was very weak. It lacked any strategy to engage supporters, voters and opponents. The IT machinery of the Congress paled in comparison to the BJP's huge IT cell. Less was spoken by Congress leaders, and there were more trolls to chase them. They never learnt from the BJP and AAP about how to generate social media buzz in their favour.

Instead, Congress leaders were accused of tampering the number of followers on Facebook. Later, all of Congress's leaders, big and small, were forced to take to social media. But they did it in the same way that they used to do so many other things. There was no seriousness and enthusiasm, and shortcuts were taken. Then there were accusations of Congress leader Ashok Gehlot tampering his Facebook page. The BJP alleged that the CM had bought 'likes' in bulk from IT firms in Istanbul, to project popularity.[24] 'Gehlotji more popular in Istanbul?' asked BJP's then national spokesperson Nirmala Sitharaman.[25] Then, it was revealed that the majority of Digvijaya Singh and Ajay Maken's fans were from Turkey. It is apparent that they were using the services of such organizations that manipulated 'likes' to produce a large number of followers in a short period of time.[26]

---

[24]'Why Do So Many People Suddenly like Ashok Gehlot's Facebook Page?' *India Today*, 10 July 2013, http://tinyurl.com/2urdfx9y. Accessed on 15 February 2024.

[25]Ghosh, Deepshikha, 'Rajasthan Chief Minister Ashok Gehlot Accused of Buying Facebook "Likes" from Istanbul', *NDTV*, 10 July 2013, http://tinyurl.com/4assbbbh. Accessed on 15 February 2024.

[26]'Facebook Politics: Istanbul "Likes" Indian Politicians, Ajay Maken More Popular in Turkey than India', *The Economic Times*, 22 August 2013, http://tinyurl.com/5n8fmxt7. Accessed on 15 February 2024.

The same had happened with the Congress-led union government. Despite having all of the resources, the UPA-led central government avoided social media. After PM Manmohan Singh denied to open an account, the decision was then made to open the Prime Minister's Office (PMO) account. But it was not a simple task. The security limitations on using the Internet from the government system were so rigorous that you couldn't click on any external links. To open this Twitter account, the then communications adviser to the PMO, Pankaj Pachauri, had to use his personal Gmail ID. Pachauri claims that the PM had specifically instructed that no further funds would be used for this work.[27] When the Nirbhaya protests began, it was expected that things would change. Things did change, although at a considerably slower rate than was expected or required.

The overall challenge was significantly larger. The most challenging task was convincing every government department to use social media. It was difficult to persuade the bureaucratic system, which used to run files behind closed doors, to face the all-around open world of social media. But there weren't many choices. Later, all of these government agencies, including the PMO, used social media in their typical manner. These were used for one-way communication. They prepared and distributed a press release or statement to the media. Social media necessitates constant engagement. This couldn't happen.

Why the Congress could not grasp the importance of social media is a mystery in and of itself. This is one of the numerous difficulties that led to the Congress leadership's defeat in the 2014 general elections.

And now, as the next general election approaches, the Congress has attempted to enhance its IT team. Its IT cell, led by party spokesman Supriya Shrinate, has already begun responding directly and quickly to BJP and other Opposition party attacks.

---

[27]Personal interview with Pankaj Pachauri

Simultaneously, it is also attacking the opponents.[28] The Congress IT cell's newfound activism has made the battle for the upcoming general elections more interesting.

Other parties, too, which were initially sceptical of using social media recognized the need of interacting with people on social media. Some realized it before and some after Narendra Modi became Prime Minister. Bihar's leader, Lalu Yadav, was previously famous for saying, '*Yeh IT-YT kya hota hai* (What is this IT-YT)?' Later, he joined Twitter, and his tweets became more frequent.[29] Almost all the leaders and parties are currently on Twitter. They frequently take selfies in the ground zero of their politics and post the pictures on social media. They themselves post information about their tours.[30]

The 2019 general elections saw the widespread and imaginative use of digital media and technology. Political parties made great use of digital media for campaign strategy and voter mobilization. This broad use of digital media was fuelled by the fact that over half of India's 900 million eligible voters had Internet and social media access. Many observers dubbed the election the 'WhatsApp' election because of the unprecedented 300 million Facebook users and over 200 million WhatsApp users, which outnumbered those in other countries.[31]

---

[28]'Congress Appoints Supriya Shrinate as New Social Media Head', *e4m*, 20 June 2022, http://tinyurl.com/mtvkrmk6. Accessed on 15 February 2024.

[29]Kumar, Madan, 'Watch Out: Lalu to Write Book on Self', *The Times of India*, 18 June 2014, http://tinyurl.com/5dt39ctt. Accessed on 15 February 2024.

[30]Chopra, Shaili, *The Big Connect: Politics in the Age of Social Media*, Random House Publishers, 2014.

[31]Sen, Ronojoy, Katharina Naumann and Vani Swarupa Murali, 'The Impact of Digital Media on the 2019 Indian General Election', *KAS*, 19 December 2019, http://tinyurl.com/ypn8rxc5. Accessed on 15 February 2024.

THE NEXT ROUND

The 2020 Delhi Assembly elections saw substantial usage of social media by all three major parties: the AAP, the Congress and the BJP. According to a report by *The Economic Times*, all of these parties spent heavily on platforms such as Facebook. The AAP spent ₹42.7 lakh on Facebook ads in the month leading up to the election in early February, while the BJP spent ₹21.5 lakh and the Congress spent ₹16.2 lakh. For this election, the AAP also enlisted the help of the Prashant Kishor-led I-PAC. It spent ₹13.6 on the 'Lage Raho Kejriwal' campaign.[32] According to an *India Today* analysis, the AAP was the largest spender on Facebook ads during that election.[33]

Arvind Kejriwal understood that his party will not be able to compete with the BJP in terms of money or muscle power. BJP deployed many CMs[34], over 200 MPs[35] and thousands of workers[36] from across the country to take part in the election campaign. Along with this, the workers and resources of the Rashtriya Swayamsevak Sangh (RSS) were also involved. So, the AAP decided to concentrate its focus on social media. They had

---

[32]Venkat Ananth, and Dinesh Narayanan, '"Lage Raho Kejriwal" vs "Dil Mein Modi": How AAP & BJP Are Fighting Digital Poll War', *The Economic Times*, 4 February 2020, http://tinyurl.com/csx6m3wk. Accessed on 15 February 2024.

[33]Rampal, Nikhil, 'No "Aam Aadmi" Party This! AAP's Facebook Campaign Four Times Costlier than BJP', *India Today*, 4 February 2020, http://tinyurl.com/yc5vr6by. Accessed on 15 February 2024.

[34]PTI, 'Delhi Elections 2020: BJP Launches Multi-Pronged Attack on AAP with Battery of Leaders; Kejriwal Counters with Jansabhas', *The Times of India*, 31 January 2020, http://tinyurl.com/3v96najm. Accessed on 15 February 2024.

[35]Snehanshu, Shekhar, 'Over 200 BJP MPs to Woo Delhi Voters', *India Today*, 5 February 2020, http://tinyurl.com/2zdxkf8r. Accessed on 15 February 2024.

[36]'Delhi Assembly Election 2020: Set for a Fight, BJP Deploys 1,800 Workers on Each Seat for Polling Day in Delhi', *Hindustan Times*, 8 February 2020, http://tinyurl.com/mryywps8. Accessed on 15 February 2024.

a clear strategy in mind. The AAP social media strategist Ankit Lal told the PTI: 'Especially in an urban constituency like Delhi, it is very important to have a well-defined social media strategy. We have been blessed that we have been frontrunners in that. [...] About 200 volunteers from across the globe comprise the core team working on different social media platforms for content creation and ideation for the Delhi Assembly polls.'[37]

According to a *Hindustan Times* story, the AAP had already prepared a force of 15,000 social media 'warriors' for this purpose. They were always prepared to refute any propaganda.[38]

This is not to say that the AAP was exclusively defensive; it also employed certain attacking strategies. They went after the Delhi BJP President Manoj Tiwari. He was targeted using numerous jokes, songs and memes. Many of them were only available in Bhojpuri. His song 'Rinkiya ke Papa' was frequently used to mock him.[39] The AAP also had a lengthy list of accomplishments to brag about on social media. All of these tricks worked, and the AAP bagged 62 out of 70 seats securing a landslide victory in the Assembly.

INFLUENCERS IN POLITICS

As Rahul Gandhi started his voyage from Kanyakumari to Kashmir during the Bharat Jodo Yatra, it became clear that the Yatra would not receive much attention in the mainstream media.

---

[37]PTI, 'Delhi Assembly Election 2020: Social Media Battle Hots up as BJP, Congress Attempt to Breach "Kejri Wall"', *Firstpost.*, 12 January 2020, http://tinyurl.com/mr3wezrt. Accessed on 15 February 2024.

[38]Jeelani, Ghulam, '15K AAP Workers to Counter Fake News on Social Media, Ahead of 2019 Lok Sabha Elections', *Hindustan Times*, 13 November 2018, http://tinyurl.com/5af4hjvr. Accessed on 15 February 2024.

[39]Vardhan, Anand, 'AAP Making Fun of Manoj Tiwari's Bhojpuri Work Betrays Cultural Insensitivity', *newslaundry*, 21 January 2020, http://tinyurl.com/2p8u9vt4. Accessed on 14 February 2024.

The Congress leadership then sought to use other mediums to get the message of Bharat Jodo Yatra to the people. The solution was found on social media. At several points along the trip, Rahul Gandhi was introduced to various influencers. The interviews or collaborations with these influencers became a success.

Some of these influencers didn't necessarily create political content. It was a well-thought-out move, as it added to making Rahul a leader of the people, accessible to all. He featured on *Curly Tales* with culinary and travel blogger Kamiya Jani in one interview.[40]

While on the road, he spoke with those who created political vlogs as well. He chatted with *Mashable India's* Siddharth Alambayan.[41] But his chat with Samdish (from *UNFILTERED by Samdish Bhatia*) was the most talked about.[42] Nearly five million people watched the interview, which was conducted in an informal and off-the-cuff style. Because of these influencers, Rahul's long journey was always in the spotlight, and by the time he arrived in Delhi, the situation was such that even mainstream television networks found it difficult to ignore him.

The BJP, of course, wasn't very far away. The campaigning for the Assembly elections in four states and Gandhi Jayanti in 2023 coincided. Around Gandhi Jayanti every year, the PM leads a cleanliness campaign. The campaign was dubbed 'Swachhata Hi Seva' for 2023. But this campaign was a little different from the previous years. When Narendra Modi launched his cleanliness campaign shortly after becoming PM in 2014, he included a notable

---

[40]Shenoy, Sanjana, 'Rahul Gandhi: If You Tell Me to Go Somewhere, I Would Rather Go…| Curly Tales', *CurlyTales*, 23 May 2023, http://tinyurl.com/32rx9a3k. Accessed on 14 February 2024.

[41]*The Bombay Journey, Mashable India*, Facebook, 27 December 2022, http://tinyurl.com/46w5uhr2. Accessed on 19 February 2024.

[42]'My Crazy Interview with Rahul Gandhi Ft. Bharat Jodo Yatra | Samdish Bhatia', YouTube, http://tinyurl.com/yv8ah9ff. Accessed on 15 February 2024.

celebrity every time. A nationwide cleanliness mega drive on the eve of Gandhi Jayanti 2023 was led by PM Narendra Modi who was joined by fitness influencer Ankit Baiyanpuria. He uploaded a video of the PM and him on social media where both were seen cleaning while wearing blue gloves.[43]

Baiyanpuria is a social media fitness expert. He has millions of followers on Instagram and many YouTube subscribers. Fitness-obsessed adolescents flock to his videos in significant numbers. Baiyanpuria has become one of the new generation's celebrities known as 'influencers' on social media due to a large number of followers and views on his posts. At a time when large-scale preparations for elections in some states and upcoming general elections are underway, the PM's appearance with a social media influencer suggests an evolving new strategy.

When Narendra Modi was still the CM of Gujarat in 2014, after his prime ministerial bid, he was seen flying kites with Bollywood actor Salman Khan.[44] His plan of identifying himself with the new generation of youth, namely first-time voters, proved successful. Despite the fact that the magic of social media had begun even at that time, the role models of the new generation were still cinema stars and cricket players, etc. The situation has now changed after nearly 10 years. The role models of this era's first-time voter generation have shifted. This generation prefers social media over films and television. According to Dilip Cherian, 'The role of these influencers has increased significantly in the new age elections. It could be a poet, a singer or an artist from your neighbourhood. It

---

[43]'Who Is Ankit Baiyanpuria, Fitness Icon Who Joined PM in Cleanliness Drive', *NDTV*, 1 October 2023, http://tinyurl.com/57puaaur . Accessed on 15 February 2024.

[44]Ghosh, Shamik, 'Salman Khan Flies Kites with Narendra Modi, Praises Him, but No Clear Endorsement', *NDTV*, 14 January 2014, http://tinyurl.com/4paty6d3. Accessed on 15 February 2024.

is critical that you find just the right type of influencer.'[45]

This usage of influencers was evident on a variety of other levels as well. *MyGov* is a citizen interaction platform run by the Government of India (GoI). On the initiative taken by *MyGov*, certain senior central government ministers gave interviews to two social media influencers. Ranveer Allahbadia (@BeerBiceps) interviewed External Affairs Minister S. Jaishankar.[46] The second was Shamani who interviewed Nitin Gadkari, minister of road and transport.[47] The Congress said that the government paid influencers for these interviews.[48] These influencers clarified that no payment was made, despite the fact that the government provided tickets and lodging for them to get to and stay in Delhi.[49]

The Rajasthan government of Ashok Gehlot announced a plan to work with influencers. These influencers would be paid between ₹10,000 and ₹5 lakh to promote state government projects, based on the number of followers or subscribers they have.[50] Meanwhile, Chhattisgarh's Baghel government was preparing to connect influencers with the party. In Madhya Pradesh, the Congress was

---

[45]Personal Interview

[46]'India & International Relations, Geopolitics, Foreign Policies explained | Dr. Jaishankar | TRS 314', YouTube, http://tinyurl.com/37zta64e. Accessed on 15 February 2024.

[47]'Meet India's Most RESPECTED Politician - Nitin Gadkari On Figuring Out 93 | Raj Shamani' YouTube, http://tinyurl.com/46tmfskx. Accessed on 15 February 2024.

[48]Anand, Nisha, 'Congress' Fresh Charge at Centre over Interviews with Social Media Influencers', *Hindustan Times*, 29 June 2023, http://tinyurl.com/2865u9fw. Accessed on 15 February 2024.

[49]Kaur, Gurmehar, 'No Payment, No Tender, Just an "Opportunity": Untangling the Beerbiceps Collab with Modi Ministers', *newslaundry*, 27 June 2023, http://tinyurl.com/4ftjjh9z. Accessed on 15 February 2024.

[50]Joy, Shemin, 'Rajasthan Govt to Pay Influencers up to Rs 5 Lakh for Running Ads', *Deccan Herald*, 30 June 2023, http://tinyurl.com/mtm65yp4. Accessed on 15 February 2024.

also observed adding influencers to its election strategy.

Now, many social media stars find advantages in associating with politics. They believe that if political figures join them, their following will grow rapidly. This has also occurred. Politicians see this as a lucrative deal in many ways. For example, for interviews, such influencers are chosen who do not ask very difficult questions or raise counter-questions on any answer. Giving interviews to mainstream media journalists may pose both of these risks.

However, another issue may develop owing to this. Many of these influencers were previously known for their songs, poetry, dancing, art, health advice, street food reviews and so on, but if they join the election campaign, they will also be seen with the party label. Another fact is that many of them have already declared their political party affiliation. Political parties are not products, and political affiliation in an emotionally polarized society might cause future difficulties for some influencers. However, individuals developing election strategies never think about the long term.

THE SOCIAL MEDIA CONUNDRUM

Earlier it was thought that as the world comes closer through social media, people will be increasingly exposed to new and different ideas. It was believed that when a lot of people would come together, there would be discussions and debates that would make people tolerant towards each other. Prejudices born out of ignorance would reduce significantly, as people would become more informed. A more analytical and forward-thinking society was expected to emerge. But that has hardly been the case. In reality, the exact opposite has happened.

But why did it turn out to be the exact opposite of what most people had anticipated? The answer lies in how the social media platforms do business; it depends on their revenue model.

There's an old adage in the media that goes, 'If you don't pay for the product, you're the product.' This is true for social media. People don't pay to use social media. The firms that run social media are in the data business. The corporation that runs this media gives individuals a platform and then makes their data available to advertising and anyone else who needs it for various reasons. The more the engagement of the people, the more data the company collects, which eventually translates into greater revenue. The more viral the content, the better; the more trending the hashtags, the better.

Now, how to engage more people?

Controversial opinions get more traction on social media. Assume you put a well-known quotation from an outstanding individual or a gorgeous picture of nature. Many people will like it, and many will describe it as lovely or even extremely good. The post will most likely disappear from people's feeds after a few such exercises. On the contrary, if you say anything controversial, you will receive far more likes. Many people will also share it. This will elicit a greater number of responses. As a result, there will be counter-reactions. This frequently lasts for a long period. A controversial social media post results in increased exchange, traffic and data, all of which leads to increased revenue. The more contentious the post, the greater the potential for revenue.

FILTER BUBBLE AND ECHO CHAMBER

Such content is further expounded by two things: filter bubble and echo chamber. Social media provides you access to the world you desire. It monitors your online behaviour and keeps track of your likes, dislikes, interests, opinions and prejudices. The personalized content is then made available to you based on these criteria. Only the stuff that you love to engage with is delivered to you. This is referred to as a 'filter bubble' in social media parlance.[51]

---

[51]'How Filter Bubbles Isoate You', YouTube, 29 November 2018, http://tinyurl.com/2sfudh88. Accessed on 19 February 2024.

In politics, think of it as seeing only news and opinions that match your political stance, thus creating a limited view. If you consistently engage with conservative posts, your social media feed may prioritize showing you more conservative news, possibly excluding diverse political perspectives.

On the other hand, when you connect with only those who share your viewpoint it creates an 'echo chamber'. Such people are more likely to comment on your words. You act the same way with your friends and followers. Then, you get to speak or hear exactly what you want to say or hear. This is known as an 'echo chamber' because one's own echo can be heard everywhere. This is often the cause of social media addiction.

The main difference between a filter bubble and echo chamber is that an echo chamber is more about people surrounding themselves with like-minded individuals, reinforcing their existing beliefs through social interactions. In contrast, a filter bubble is shaped by algorithms that tailor content to individual preferences, limiting exposure to diverse viewpoints even if the user is not actively seeking them.

Filter bubble and echo chamber are the two characteristics of social media that contribute to polarization. Every alternate way of thinking is either useless or a conspiracy. Hatred towards other beliefs or ideologies arises from here as well, and can occasionally lead to viewing hate speech as normal. This is the point at which people begin to trust utterly false news and conspiracy theories. This fake news will be discussed in depth in the following chapter.

A BRIEF HISTORY OF SOCIAL MEDIA IN INDIA

By the way, social media surfaced when the smartphone was not around. Even if we exclude the early bulletin boards (Yahoo Chat and Yahoo Messenger) from this category, *SixDegrees.com* launched a new means of connecting people all over the world in 1997. It was based on Frigyes Karinthy's notion that any two persons in the globe are separated by a distance of six or fewer people. Later, such a societal association was dubbed a social network. What we now term social media was originally designed to connect people, hence it was named 'social network'. Later, as users began sharing content on such sites, it began to emerge as a media and was dubbed social media.

Orkut was the first widely used social networking site in India. When Google launched Orkut in 2004, smartphones did not exist and people used PCs and laptops to access it. Nonetheless, India and Brazil were the two countries with the highest number of visitors to this platform. However, as Facebook grew and became popular, Orkut faded away, despite the fact that it was a Google venture.

Facebook

Facebook, like Orkut, was started in 2004, but it was first limited to university students. When it later opened its doors to the public, it broke all records. It was launched in India on 26 September 2006 and within four years had more than 15 million users.[52] It also opened an office in Hyderabad the same year.[53] Furthermore, after four years of growing popularity in India, Facebook's user base surpassed 100 million in 2014.[54] At the time, it was in the Indian market that Facebook was growing at the fastest rate. This figure further reached to 380 million by 2020.[55] That is, about one-third of all adults in India had joined Facebook. Although other platforms have received more attention, Facebook's political impact has grown

[52]PTI, 'Facebook Opens Office in India', *Business Standard*, 20 January 2013, http://tinyurl.com/3kruxehy. Accessed on 15 February 2024.

[53]Ibid.

[54]Singh, Shelley, 'After Hitting 100 Million, Facebook Now Aims at 1 Billion Users in India', *The Times of India*, 8 April 2014, http://tinyurl.com/5yfb5jar. Accessed on 15 February 2024.

[55]Sircar, Sushovan, 'A 14-Year "Timeline": Facebook's Roller-Coaster India Journey', *the quint*, 25 April 2020, http://tinyurl.com/4xb2dk2r. Accessed on 15 February 2024.

as a result of its penetration into small towns and villages. Facebook was the first compulsion for politicians to engage with social media.

Twitter

Twitter is more popular among the elite or power elite. These are the people who have a big impact on political debate. According to Shivam Shankar Singh, 'There aren't many ordinary people on Twitter, and there aren't many votes on Twitter. However, it is a forum where an idea can be germinated and spread. Plenty of debates begin on Twitter.'[56]

But it was Twitter that wielded the most political power around the world. Whether it is governments, heads of state, all major leaders, journalists, intellectuals, political parties and party spokespersons from around the world—if they register their attendance anywhere regularly, it is solely on Twitter. It is regarded as the most effective medium for connecting with and reaching out to a broader audience. In 2022, almost 23.6 million Indians were using Twitter. Prime Minister Narendra Modi's name is prominent among them. If we look at the global scale, he is ranked eighth in the world based on the number of followers.[57] He currently has over 95 million followers on Twitter and is far ahead of Amitabh Bachchan, Virat Kohli and Sachin Tendulkar in terms of number of followers.

Twitter is unique among social media platforms in that it lacks a system for issuing and accepting friend requests. Anyone can follow anyone else and tag anyone with a tweet. Like other forms of social media, it is a tremendous equalizer, putting big and small, strong and powerless people on the same footing. Twitter captures this attitude significantly better than most other

---

[56]Personal interview with Shivam Shankar Singh

[57]Srinivas, Eshita, 'Musk to Modi: A Look at the Faces behind the Most-Followed Twitter Accounts of 2023', *Lifestyle Asia*, 31 March 2023, http://tinyurl.com/mkr29k7u. Accessed on 19 February 2024.

social media sites. Anyone can use this to contact the PM or the president about any little issue. It compelled all government departments to respond to queries from the public. It was a form of empowerment for ordinary people.

Nobody expected Twitter to become so powerful when it first began in 2006. It was launched as a microblogging platform. You could only post 140 characters on it. People mistook it for a social media version of SMS. Through it, the world soon discovered the power of one-liners. Politicians who used to speak in great detail quickly learnt the art of being brief.

YouTube

YouTube transformed social media in a different way. Anyone can now create their own videos and broadcast them to YouTube, drawing viewers from all around the world. Not only can you share videos made there, but you can also create your own channel. YouTube grew in popularity during the time when practically every second or third hand had a smartphone with a camera capable of shooting extremely good broadcast-grade videos. Then there were free apps available that made video and audio editing a piece of cake. Anyone can now become an anchor or host a debate on any topic from the comfort of their home. It also provided a platform for those whose voices had previously gone unheard, or for those who were unable to find their way into the mainstream media. From this point on, the concept of citizen journalism took hold.

Around 30,000 hours of new videos are uploaded on YouTube every hour.[58] Their exact number is impossible to determine. With the average video being 11.7 minutes long, there could be around 9.36 billion minutes of video content hosted on YouTube. That's 156 million hours of content. It would take more than 17,000 years

[58]Wise, Jason, 'How Many Videos Are Uploaded to YouTube a Day in 2024?', *EARTHWEB*, 5 February 2024, http://tinyurl.com/37ptnh8y. Accessed on 15 February 2024.

to watch every minute of video on the platform.[59] YouTube just offers videos, but it has become the second largest search engine after Google. When a lot of people want to find anything or learn more about something, they go straight to YouTube.

YouTube arrived in India in 2008, three years after its introduction, and the number of users in India increased to 225 million over the next 10 years. On this occasion, Google's then South Asia Vice President Ranjan Anandan stated that YouTube reaches 85 per cent of highly engaged Internet users over the age of 18 in India.[60] This figure has steadily increased since then. As a result, even conventional television news outlets are paying increasing attention to YouTube. It is no longer possible to ignore it in politics or business.

There are numerous additional social media sites that all play a part in politics. While there are many like Instagram, Reddit and others, the most important one to mention is WhatsApp. WhatsApp began as a messenger, not as a social media site. It was, in some ways, a better and more modern version of SMS in which not only large messages but also images, audio, movies and other media can be sent. Along with this, enormous groups can be formed by adding many people to it, resembling social media in certain ways. It launched later than other social media networks. It quickly rose to prominence in politics and fake news after its initial launch in 2009. This role of WhatsApp will be discussed separately later in this book.

---

[59]West, Chloe, '49 YouTube Stats 2023: Engagement, Views, Revenue (And More)', *Descript*, 14 August 2023, http://tinyurl.com/yjt8rrzw. Accessed on 29 February 2024.

[60]IANS, '80% Indian Internet Users across All Age-Groups Browse YouTube: Google', *Business Standard*, 23 March 2018, http://tinyurl.com/3tw7xhe6. Accessed on 19 February 2024.

5

FAKE NEWS AS A POLITICAL STRATEGY

In 1967, India was electing its fourth Lok Sabha. Colonel Ved Rattan Mohan, the chairman of Mohan Meakin, a prominent liquor manufacturer in India, secured a Congress ticket for the Lucknow seat.[1] Colonel Mohan, who built the famous India rum brand Old Monk, was a well-known figure in both politics and business. Also, the rich industrialist had no paucity of resources for a successful campaign. There were other reasons also that made it seem like Mohan's victory was almost inevitable. The Lok Sabha constituency of Lucknow was the traditional seat of the Congress, and while the Congress was looking a little weak throughout the entire country, the Lucknow seat seemed unaffected by that wind.

Another significant factor in that election was the absence of Atal Bihari Vajpayee, the most popular leader of the Bharatiya Jana Sangh, who had lost two successive elections from the Lucknow Lok Sabha constituency in 1957 and 1962.[2] Vajpayee's decision to not run from Lucknow, where he used to gather large crowds with his impassioned speeches, was also reassuring for the Congress.

Colonel Mohan's sole viable opponent was Anand Narain Mulla. He was an Urdu poet as well as a lawyer and an

---

[1]*Statistical Report on General Elections, 1967 to the Fourth Lok Sabha, Volume I*, Election Commission of India, 1968.

[2]Vajpayee contested 1957 election from two seats Lucknow and Mathura.

intellectual.[3] He was contesting the election as an independent candidate. Even though he was not as famous as his competitor, he had some following. But it seemed impossible for an independent candidate to compete with the organizational strength of the Congress and Colonel Mohan's personal status.

Narain faced an additional challenge. His past was acting against him. His father, Jagat Narain Mulla, was a prosecutor in the well-known Kakori railway robbery case in 1925, where revolutionaries like Chandra Shekhar Azad, Rajendra Lahiri, Ram Prasad Bismil and Ashfaqullah were involved. Narain had assisted his father on the case. And this incident had not gone away from public memory. The worry was that Anand Narain Mulla might face negative publicity related to the Kakori case during the election campaign.

But an unfounded rumour shifted the wind at the last second. The rumour began to circulate that the Congress candidate was campaigning while inebriated. A narrative was built that the Congress had handed the ticket to an alcoholic from Lucknow. The Congress employed all of its resources, all of the country's major leaders visited and a large sum of money was spent at the time. Nothing, however, could refute this rumour-fuelled narrative. When the election results were announced, Anand Narain Mulla won easily. This was the first election in which the Congress lost the Lucknow seat.[4] The following election saw the Congress recapture the seat again.

This Lucknow election demonstrates that what we call 'fake news' now is not a novel concept. Through rumours and fake news, dirty politics has ruined the game of elections. Even back then, carrying out character assasination and smear campaigns was

---

[3]Ali, Zaheer, *Poet of Humanity: Life and Works of Anand Narain Mulla*, Aakar Books, 2023.

[4]*Statistical Report on General Elections, 1967 to the Fourth Lok Sabha, Volume I*, Election Commission of India, 1968.

rampant. Political ethics were ignored in order to win elections. However, in the second decade of the twenty-first century, these practices have reached unprecedented heights. The menace of fake news is wreaking havoc.

THE SUDDEN UPTICK IN FAKE NEWS

For a long time, information has been recognized as a powerful weapon in the hands of wicked individuals. Propaganda, manipulative information and information designed to intimidate and force people into doing specific actions were known to mankind even before the rise of information technology and its rapid development. However, in modern times, technology allows misinformation to travel swiftly and poses greater risks.

During the period of traditional channels—press, television and radio—information was subjected to numerous checks before being shared, as publishers, channels and providers might have been held liable for what was communicated if it turned out to be false or defamatory. However, it's not the same when it comes to online sources of information. Anyone may start a blog, post on their Facebook page and share whatever they want on Instagram or Twitter. People are much more immersed in this online realm; we spend hours online—on public transport, during breaks at work and when we go home and decide to totally immerse ourselves in Internet browsing. We are constantly bombarded with information online and may not always have the energy or time to determine what is genuine and what is not.

Recent spate of political fake news or disinformation in India began in 2012 when PM Manmohan Singh's government was rapidly losing credibility. Another theory holds that the government's credibility suffered as a result of fake news. On the one hand, anti-government movements such as IAC was gaining traction, while the BJP's caravan was marching confidently towards Delhi. By the time the 2014 general elections came around, the spread of fake news had reached new heights.

We arrived at a crossroads where the collision of dirty politics and lightning-fast dissemination technologies was made possible by mobile technology. This unholy union has fundamentally altered the character of politics. Previously irregular at the local level, the politics of rumours, fake news and character assassinations can now be done on a massive scale and in a coordinated manner at the national level. What was earlier muttered in a shrouded manner can now be conveyed to each home and person. What had previously been a political disease has now become a pandemic.

There are sociological reasons for this as well. We have arrived at a point in history when emotions have trumped facts—the post-truth era. The Oxford Dictionary defines 'post-truth' as 'relating to or denoting circumstances in which objective facts are less influential in shaping public opinion than appeals to emotion and personal belief'. [5] People have begun to build their beliefs based on emotional appeal rather than truth and reality. They have become dissatisfied with the idioms of liberal democratic politics and started looking for alternatives. People's trust in many of democracy's essential institutions has begun to dwindle for a variety of reasons. The resulting vacuum enables conservative and revivalist forces to get a foothold. The groundwork has now been laid for the societal polarization for which these forces have been working for years. Even while the commercial media was profiting financially, its credibility was dwindling. And this was not limited to India, but has occurred around the world.

Politicians have also made significant contributions to shaping this impression. When news does not favour them, they quickly label it as fake news. Once, former US President Donald Trump

[5]'The Surprising Origins of "Post-truth"—And How It Was Spawned by the Liberal Left', *The Conversation*, 18 November 2016, http://tinyurl.com/mwfvf5m6. Accessed on 15 February 2024.

accused CNN of being 'fake news' so as to avoid answering difficult questions.[6]

In the post-truth era, it has become excruciatingly difficult to distinguish between what is real and what is fake. Even those who are considered to be informed often fall in the trap of fake news, and also spread it further. An example will help us comprehend the impact of this. For several decades, efforts have been carried out through whispers and stories to persuade people that Indira Gandhi's husband, Feroze Gandhi, was a Muslim.[7] However, for a long time, people did not pay attention to such things and it was simply dismissed as hearsay. However, in the last decade and a half, the number of people who believe in this has risen dramatically. Such people will often be seen participating in debates on television news channels. Many such notions are getting ingrained in people's brains that have nothing to do with the reality.

When mobile phones and smartphones became available to everyone, politics gained a new instrument for creating narratives on the basis of fake news. Soon after, this tool was transformed into the most powerful weapon capable of annihilating any adversary. Such a weapon can be used to set the agenda of both society and politics. Fake news was crafted in such a way that it went viral and reinforced a specific narrative. The short-term goal of the fake news generated for political advantage is to win elections. The long-term goal is to develop a society with a specific ideology and prejudice; a society that thinks and reacts in a certain way on every key occasion. Some trends of the country's fake news era, which began around the year 2012, are quite apparent.

---

[6]Slack, Donovan, 'Trump to CNN: "You Are Fake News"', *USAToday*, 11 January 2017, http://tinyurl.com/34vx8mtz. Accessed on 15 January 2024.

[7]Ahmad, Mobeen, 'Was Indira Gandhi's Husband Feroze Gandhi a Muslim? Read Fact-Check', *DFrac*, 19 August 2022, http://tinyurl.com/2ex4u2fs. Accessed on 15 January 2024.

A POLARIZED WORLD

Political polarization during elections involves the deliberate attempt by a political party to intensify the conviction among its supporters that their party is correct, while portraying the opposing party as responsible for all shortcomings in the country. This strategy aims to solidify the party's support base and can lead followers to view the opposing party as the cause of various issues. Additionally, political polarization serves to offer voters simplified decision-making guides, known as 'voting heuristics', which assist political parties in rallying their supporters.

What is heuristics? Imagine you're at a grocery store with a large number of different cereals to choose from. Instead of analysing every detail of each brand, you might use shortcuts, like grabbing familiar brands, choosing the cereal based on health claims or picking the cheapest option. Such shortcuts are called heuristics, and we use them in voting too. They help us navigate complex elections with limited time and easily available information.

Fake news has played the most key part in spreading and strengthening polarization everywhere. When it comes to social media, we've seen it exacerbate polarization in practically every country on the planet. Wherever a divide was noticed, social media enlarged it and turned it into a ditch. In India, polarization has taken several forms, the most common of which is sectarianism. In most regions, this polarization took the shape of Hindu and Muslim binary, but other sorts of divisions were also not spared. Like in Manipur, the same polarization game was played between the Meitei and Kuki communities.

Fake news becomes monstrous when it comes into contact with sectarian narratives and political strategies at the same time. There have always been radical sections in both the Hindu and Muslim communities that have attempted to demonize members of the other community. However, such people were mainly on the fringes of society, and their impact on the rest of society was minor. But the age of social media and fake news has had such an influence that these elements are no longer on the fringe; they have reached the mainstream and begun to sway a wide segment of society.

On social media, all Muslims are quickly labelled as traitors or as a community whose members are constantly engaged in 'jihad'. They are seen as people who have a large number of children and are constantly looking for ways to convert individuals of other religions. Many terms have been coined to describe this, including 'love jihad', 'land jihad', 'narcotic jihad' and 'train jihad'.

For this, a conspiracy theory that India will soon become a Muslim country is bolstered, and we are told that Hindus must wake up to prevent this from happening. Various justifications are advanced in support of this, and fear is instilled. According to one such tweet, 11 crore Rohingya Muslims from Myanmar have infiltrated India in order to turn it into a Muslim country. While the truth is that Myanmar's overall population is less than 60 million, with Muslims constituting approximately 4 per cent of the population.[8] The most alarming thing about this is that, with the emergence of social media, the number of such ordinary individuals who began to believe in this has swiftly expanded. Many of our current problems stem from this.

WHEN FAKE NEWS SPILLS BLOOD

Fake news that spreads hatred is not limited to social media. Soon after, on-ground activism in response to this fabricated news began to emerge. Hatred rarely stays restricted to the mind for long before it manifests itself on the ground. In many places, people have been led to believe that cows are being slaughtered illegally. In response to this, large active 'Gau Rakshaks' or 'Cow

---

[8]Sinha, Pratik, Sumaiya Shaikh and Arjun Sidharath (eds), *India Misinformed: The True Story*, Harper Collins Publishers India, 2019.

Vigilantes' organizations have emerged in various parts of North India. In several places, people transporting livestock were lynched on the grounds that they were bringing cows for slaughter.[9]

A mob massacred Mohammad Akhlaq and his son in Dadri, UP, on the suspicion that the meat kept in their refrigerator was beef.[10] Fake news has sparked riots and killed people in many locations. Hate slogans were raised on multiple occasions for the first time in independent India. Videos of offensive chants such as 'Jab mu**e kaate jayenge, wo Ram Ram chillayenge' were widely circulated.[11] Even the most fanatical adherents could not utter such phrases, at least publicly, two decades ago.

Aside from that, the front that saw the most activism was the 'love jihad' issue. It's an old allegation that Muslim males seduce Hindu girls, marry them and convert them to Islam. According to the love jihad conspiracy theory, these attempts are being conducted on an organized level to make India an Islamic country. Love jihad is typically discussed only when the boy is Muslim and the girl is Hindu. If the reverse is true, those who discuss love jihad mostly remain silent. This conspiracy theory has had such an impact that laws have been enacted in numerous states to prohibit it.[12] When there were a lot of outcries in UP in 2014, Union Home Minister Rajnath Singh stated that he has no idea

---

[9]Chatterji, Saubhadra, 'In the Name of Cow: Lynching, Thrashing, Condemnation in Three Years of BJP Rule', *Hindustan Times*, 19 July 2017, http://tinyurl.com/yt5ewt39. Accessed on 15 February 2024.

[10]Kumar, Abhimanyu, 'The Lynching That Changed India', *Aljazeera*, 5 October 2017, http://tinyurl.com/mv4h3mst. Accessed on 15 February 2024.

[11]Zaffar, Hanan, and Hasan Akram, 'Anti-muslim Slogans Raised in Indian Capital, Suspects in Custody', *Aljazeera*, 10 August 2021, http://tinyurl.com/yebh6698. Accessed on 15 February 2024.

[12]Banerjee, Tirtho, 'Why Maharashtra Wants to Join States That Have Laws against "Love Jihad"', *India Today*, 28 December 2022, http://tinyurl.com/28hs9e4z. Accessed on 15 February 2024.

what love jihad is.[13] However, he later appeared to oppose love jihad, like all other BJP leaders.

Interfaith marriage was once considered a progressive idea and was viewed with great respect, but it is now villainized. The anti-love jihad activities and newly established legislation strip away to a large extent the right that gave girls the freedom to choose their life partner; a right that they have only begun to get. In love jihad, patriarchy discovered new means to strengthen itself. The issue did not end there; a demand was made in the Gujarat Legislative Assembly to pass a legislation requiring any love marriage to be done only with the permission of the parents.[14]

There have been other conspiracy theories that have misled people to stoke the unfounded fears of Muslims trying to take over the country by increasing the community's population.

Character assassination is the most aggressive form of fake news after the Hindu–Muslim divide. This type of character assassination is not confined to current political figures. People from practically every era of history have also been targeted. Although Jawaharlal Nehru was the most prominent target, even Mahatma Gandhi was not spared. Several falsehoods were spread about both of them. Rumours of Nehru's clothing being laundered in Paris were getting old.[15] This time, an entire tale was made up that Nehru's predecessors were actually Muslims who disguised themselves to fool the nation.[16] Because Nehru's name was

---

[13]PTI, 'As BJP Rakes up "Love Jihad" in UP, Rajnath Singh Says He Has "No Idea about It"', *The Times of India*, 12 September 2014, http://tinyurl.com/yhxdjbta. Accessed on 15 February 2024.

[14]'Gujarat MLAs: Make Consent of Parents Mandatory for Love Marriages', *The Times of India*, 17 March 2023, http://tinyurl.com/mwdamufy. Accessed on 15 February 2023.

[15]'Nightmare of Nehruism—A "Tribute" to Jawahar Lal Nehru by Sita Ram Goel', *OPIndia*, 27 May 2020, http://tinyurl.com/4eexjc99. Accessed on 15 February 2024.

[16]Saha, Abhishek, 'Truth about Nehru: Why Conspiracy Theorists Are Wrong about Him', *Hindustan Times*, 9 July 2015, http://tinyurl.com/4j2xp6pc. Accessed on 15 February 2024.

associated with many of the achievements of independent India, certain groups felt it was important to diminish his reputation.

Sardar Patel and Subhas Chandra Bose were pitted against Nehru. Despite some minor difference, all of the facts and even documents reveal that Nehru and Patel had a very good relationship. However, in fake news, we encounter a Nehru who was conspiring against Patel. Furthermore, despite all of the accessible images and press reports, it was said that Nehru did not even attend Patel's cremation when he died.[17]

This narrative has been told many times: Subhas Chandra Bose was alive when India gained freedom, and Nehru did not allow him to come to India. Many conspiracy theories have been put forward for this. Not only that, but the fake news factory published a false letter in which Nehru is claimed to have referred to Subhas Chandra Bose as a war criminal.[18] When PM Narendra Modi took office in 2014, he vowed that all confidential documents pertaining to Netaji would be made public. A government website called *Netaji Papers* was also set up for this purpose, in which all Netaji-related files were posted one by one. But no such thing in any of these documents could besiege Nehru. However, the spread of false information about Nehru and Netaji continues to this day.[19]

Fake news wagers are placed not only on historical figures but also on current politicians. This has affected all the country's leaders, including Narendra Modi, Sonia Gandhi, Rahul Gandhi, Digvijaya Singh, Akhilesh Yadav, Yogi Adityanath and Arvind

---

[17]Ramaseshan, Radhika, 'Prasad Funeral Jibe at Nehru', *The Telegraph online*, 31 October 2013, http://tinyurl.com/mrxdu77j. Accessed on 16 February 2024.

[18]Talukdar, Sreemoy, '"War Criminal": How Did a "Fake" Letter about Netaji Bose Create So Much Controversy?', *Firstpost.*, 25 January 2016, http://tinyurl.com/yc7xyrkr. Accessed on 16 February 2024.

[19]Saha, Abhishek, 'Netaji Bose vs Nehru: Political Rivalry or Historical Myth?', *Hindustan Times*, 15 April 2015, http://tinyurl.com/46j8ke8c. Accessed on 16 February 2024.

Kejriwal. Of course, this list is not exhaustive. The more powerful the leaders are, the more vulnerable they are to fake news. According to a fake report, Congress leader Sonia Gandhi was formerly a bar dancer in Italy.[20]According to another fake news a former CBI director gave a statement that Narendra Modi is the country's most corrupt leader. Then we have Yogi Adityanath's statement, where he says that his goal is to safeguard the cow, not women.[21] In the end, no one is spared by fake news.

Photoshop and deep fake videos have become the two most important tools for character assassination. Political fake news factories that popped up around the country quickly realized that by combining two separate images, they could generate a new story. There is an archival snapshot of Mahatma Gandhi and Jawaharlal Nehru talking to each other during a meeting. Jawaharlal Nehru was ingeniously removed from the photograph, and a barely dressed dancer was made to take his place.[22]

Similarly, PM Narendra Modi had travelled to Argentina in 2018 to attend the G-20 summit. During that visit, FIFA President Gianni Infantino gave him a football jersey. While the original jersey said, 'Modi G-20', the fabricated one had it changed to 'Modi 420'. This 'G' was cleverly deleted and replaced with the number '4'.[23] Similarly, a photo showing Narendra Modi garlanding the

---

[20]Kumar Jha, Abhishek, '"Italian Bar Dancer", "Bar Girl in India" Google Search Shows Sonia Gandhi', *TECHWORM*, 8 January 2024, http://tinyurl.com/axp69rup. Accessed on 16 February 2024.

[21]Chattopadhyay, Aditi, 'Fact Check: Did Yogi Adityanath Say It Is His Job to Save Cows, Not Women?', *The Logical Indian*, 2 October 2020, http://tinyurl.com/2jdbs3vr. Accessed on 16 February 2024.

[22]Varma, Aishwarya, 'Edited Image of Mahatma Gandhi Shared to Take a Dig at Late Leader', *the quint*, 4 October 2021, http://tinyurl.com/mu5sxy4f. Accessed on 16 February 2024.

[23]Jha, Priyanka, 'Viral: Photoshopped Image of Football Jersey with "Modi 420" Written on It', *alt news*, 4 December 2018, http://tinyurl.com/3xuhzbs4. Accessed on 16 February 2024.

statue of Mahatma Gandhi's murderer Nathuram Godse was released, despite the fact that it was a photoshop trick. He was actually garlanding Pandit Deen Dayal Upadhyaya's statue.[24]

Photoshop isn't always required. The work can be done solely by a false caption on a photo as well. A photograph of someone touching Sonia Gandhi's feet was circulated with the caption: 'Prime Minister Manmohan Singh touching Sonia's feet.'[25] Alternatively, a black and white photograph of a girl in a swimsuit was said to be Sonia Gandhi's photograph.[26] Another one is where an image shows PM Narendra Modi laughing, and the text states that he was laughing at the death of former PM Atal Bihari Vajpayee.[27]

The finest instance of video editing is a statement by Rahul Gandhi, in which he is heard saying, 'I will set up a factory where you put potatoes in one side and gold comes out the other.' Even now, this video is frequently shared to demonstrate Rahul Gandhi's folly. However, the truth was quite different. Rahul Gandhi had stated in his original address, 'Modi ji claims that I will set up a factory in which from one side...' The portion saying, 'Modi Ji claims' has been removed from the edited video.[28]

---

[24]Deodia, Arjun, 'Fact Check: False Claim Saying Modi Pays Tribute to Godse Resurfaces', *India Today*, 18 January 2020, http://tinyurl.com/yw8zxft5. Accessed on 16 February 2024.

[25]'Fact Check: Does This Photo Show Manmohan Singh Touching Sonia Gandhi's Feet?', *The Times of India*, 29 March 2023, http://tinyurl.com/2y62bnby. Accessed on 20 February 2024.

[26]Deodia, Arjun, 'Fact Check: Bond Girl in Bikini Passed off as Sonia Gandhi', *India Today*, 24 June 2020, http://tinyurl.com/9bcymy5m. Accessed on 16 February 2024.

[27]Sinha, Pratik, Sumaiya Shaikh and Arjun Sidharath (eds), *India Misinformed: The True Story*, Harper Collins Publishers India, 2019.

[28]Ibid.

FAKING GLORY

Fake news has been used not only to assassinate individuals, but also to glorify leaders. For example, there has been a lot of false claims hailing PM Modi. Fake news told us that according to a bureaucrat, Narendra Modi works between 18 and 20 hours every day.[29] Quotes from world leaders praising Modi are shown. It's also said that according to Julian Assange, the founder of WikiLeaks, Narendra Modi is the world's most uncorruptible leader.[30] Then we see an image from the G-20 summit in which Narendra Modi is sitting on a chair in the centre and several international leaders, including then US President Donald Trump, are listening to his advice. When the original photograph was revealed, it was discovered that chair was actually empty.[31] Interestingly, in Russia, President Vladimir Putin was made to sit on the same chair on which Modi was made to sit in India.[32] Fake news brigades think alike no matter where they are.

All of these posts of admiration lasted only a few days before disappearing. However, posts of character assassination or propaganda against someone never go away; they are heard and seen repeatedly. This brings us to another aspect of the fake news. In this, a falsehood told for condemnation or character assassination is more durable than a lie told for praise, and it has a much higher circulation value and longer shelf life.

If we want to understand how disinformation and fake news entered politics and what it does, we should listen to Amit Shah's 2018 speech in Kota, Rajasthan. He delivered this address to

---

[29]Ibid.

[30]PTI, 'Never Said Narendra Modi Incorruptible: Wikileaks', *The Economic Times*, 18 March 2014, http://tinyurl.com/35ejx38a. Accessed on 16 February 2024.

[31]Sinha, Pratik, Sumaiya Shaikh and Arjun Sidharath (eds), *India Misinformed: The True Story*, Harper Collins Publishers India, 2019.

[32]Evans, Patrick, 'Vladimir Putin: The President Who Wasn't There', *BBC News*, 10 July 2017, http://tinyurl.com/3yr8ch4d. Accessed on 16 February 2024.

BJP's Internet volunteers, just as the Assembly elections were approaching. He describes how the party has added lakhs of individuals to WhatsApp groups in UP. A single communication, whether accurate or misleading, reaches millions of people in one stroke. He then told an anecdote. One day, a UP worker spread the word that CM Akhilesh Yadav had slapped his father, Mulayam Singh. This news was absolutely false. Akhilesh and Mulayam Singh were 600 km apart at the time the incident was reported. Yet, the story went viral and favoured the BJP. Amit Shah also stated that this is improper and should not be done.[33]

The speech by Amit Shah highlights that a lot of fake news business is going on with the knowledge of political parties. When the IT cells of the parties and their in-charge are spotted propagating fake news, there is little doubt left. On Twitter, party leaders and even the PM are frequently seen following those who promote fake news.[34] Some platforms, on the other hand, are frequently formed outside of the party structure to disseminate fake news. Websites like *NITI Central* and *Postcard News* are excellent examples of this. Although both of these are now shut down, numerous more have mushroomed.[35]

In general, all fake news attempts are founded on Joseph Goebbels's (the Nazi Party's chief propagandist) view that a lie said once stays a lie, but if told a thousand times it becomes the truth. When the same things are said repeatedly in different ways and with varied examples, people begin to discuss it and

---

[33]'Shri Amit Shah Addresses Social Media Volunteers' Meet in Kota, Rajasthan: 22.09.2018', YouTube, 23 September 2018, http://tinyurl.com/25w3ksry. Accessed on 20 February 2024.

[34]Chaturvedi, Swati, *I Am a Troll: Inside the Secret World of the Bjp's Digital Army*, Juggernaut, 2016.

[35]Shankar, Saumya, 'Why Fake News is Indian Internet's Biggest Problem', *NewsClick*, 10 July 2017, http://tinyurl.com/mvcrhn33. Accessed on 16 February 2024; Sinha, Pratik, 'Postcard News: Mass Producing Fake News', *alt news*, 27 May 2017, http://tinyurl.com/23uxc8jz. Accessed on 16 February 2024.

a narrative begins to emerge. Many similar false reports have circulated in UP and Bihar, claiming that only the Yadav caste has received all of the benefits of quota for other backward castes (OBC). So many examples were offered that individuals from OBC castes other than Yadavs gradually began to believe them. After implementation of the Mandal Commission's recommendations, a powerful vote bank that had begun to grow in this part of India was destroyed solely on the basis of fake news. And the politics of these states were fundamentally altered.

The Congress held a National OBC Convention in Delhi in June 2018. During his speech at the Conference, party leader Rahul Gandhi stated that Coca-Cola was invented and launched by a lemonade vendor. The truth is that the recipe was invented by a pharmacist. And what the country's largest Opposition party's head said in this conference was actually the content of a long-circulating fake story on social media.[36]

Many other leaders, including ministers, have expressed similar things in public. But we don't expect such things from the president or PM. In many countries, they are the highest positions, and what they say is assumed to be national policy. They have a full team, from speech writers to researchers, thus we expect no errors in their talks. However, the impact of fake news is often obvious in their addresses as well. During Donald Trump's presidency, there was a lot of fake news in his remarks and speeches.[37]

The office of the PM of India also became its victim. When PM Narendra Modi was campaigning in Karnataka in 2018, during a public gathering in Bidar, he stated that when revolutionaries

---

[36]Sinha, Pratik, Sumaiya Shaikh and Arjun Sidharath (eds), *India Misinformed: The True Story*, Harper Collins Publishers India, 2019.

[37]Timm, Jane C., 'Trump versus the Truth: The Most Outrageous Falsehoods of His Presidency', *NBC News*, 31 December 2020, http://tinyurl.com/4hbhp7dk. Accessed on 16 February 2024.

like Bhagat Singh and Batukeshwar Dutt were imprisoned for protecting the country, no Congress politician went to meet them in jail. The truth is that when these revolutionaries were imprisoned in Lahore in 1929, Congress leader Jawaharlal Nehru visited them there.[38] Its news also appeared in newspapers at the time.[39] Furthermore, the cases of these revolutionaries were fought by Congress lawyers. Whatever the PM said during the public meeting in Bidar had long been spread through fake news on social media. Because this item supported many BJP preconceptions and its use against the Congress could yield positive outcomes, it was included in the PM's speech without cross checking the reality.

Politicians are not the only ones who are susceptible to the temptation to accept fake news as truth; the mainstream media is also prone to it. There are many examples of fake news that have been broadcast by television news networks. On 8 November 2016, when PM Narendra Modi declared demonetization and new ₹2,000 notes were introduced, various news outlets reported for several days that the new ₹2,000 note had a microchip. The channels also tallied its several advantages. In truth, it was fake news that jumped from social media and reached these channels. There is almost no channel that later apologized for the lies.[40]

So far, experience has shown that once the process of fake news begins in politics, it is impossible to stop or limit it. Politicians feel that the best way to combat fake news is to spread more fake news—if someone is spreading fake news

---

[38]Sinha, Pratik, Sumaiya Shaikh and Arjun Sidharath (eds), *India Misinformed: The True Story*, Harper Collins Publishers India, 2019.

[39]Balkrishna, 'Fact Check: Was Modi Right about Congress Leaders Not Meeting Bhagat Singh in Jail?', *India Today*, 18 September 2018, http://tinyurl.com/yt7w38c4. Accessed on 16 February 2024.

[40]@samjawed65, X (formerly Twitter), 8 November 2020, 11.30 a.m., http://tinyurl.com/yfa6udyr. Accessed on 20 February 2024.

about you, you should bring a flood of fake news against your opponent. Nobody knows how to put an end to this competitive streak.

FIGHTING FAKE NEWS

There have been numerous organizations, websites and media sources that have attempted to combat fake news. It is often thought that the greatest approach to fight fake news is to expose it. Bring the truth to the forefront, and fake news will lose its influence. These organizations take each piece of fake news, analyse it, flip the pages of history to prove it wrong, seek archives, do all kinds of attempts to discover the truth and then tell the full detail about how that particular news was deceptive. It's a massive task, but it is effective.

However, owing to the algorithmic nature of social media, there is no guarantee that this refutation will also reach the people who are subjected to fake news. It is very likely that it will not reach them at all. On the contrary, the folks who receive this refutation frequently do not receive any fake news at all. After receiving a rebuttal, some people begin seeking the original fake news. If you follow those who propagate fake news on social media, you will only receive fake news, and if you follow those who refute them you will only receive refutation. You can apply this adage about truth and lies to fake news as well: 'When the truth is tying its shoelaces to leave its dwelling, the falsehood came back after six rounds of the city.'

All of this, however, does not imply that exposing fake news is a futile undertaking. First of all, it sends a message to people who spread fake news that individuals who probe lies and uncover the truth are also always engaged behind the scenes. We can also derive this from the fact that fake news busters are constantly on the radar of party IT cells. Some politicians call them liars, and a troll army of political organizations is always trying to defame them. There are numerous risks associated with exposing fake news.

Alt News is the country's largest organization dedicated to combating fake news. Its co-founder, Mohammed Zubair, was imprisoned and faced numerous lawsuits as a result of his activities. When he was imprisoned, he told *The New York Times* in an interview: 'People in power want to shut me up for exposing their propaganda, their lies and their hate campaigns, they want to scare other journalists and activists by targeting me.'[41]

Fake news is more than just the fabrication of facts, deception and disinformation. It has something to do with people's preconceptions, prejudices and fallacies. You check the facts in any situation and tell the people the truth. They recognize the reality as well, but nothing else happens. Their views, prejudices and fallacies stay unchanged. In any case, perceptions are more important than facts in what we term the post-truth era. The mentality that gives fake news a stronghold in society cannot be changed by fact-checking only. In the TED lecture series, American journalist Robert Hernandez said something very essential to us about this: 'We can be persuaded by what we see even though we know that it's fake.'[42]

Rahul Matthan, an attorney specializing in technology, media and telecommunications law, put it another way:

> Fake news operates at the confluence of precisely engineered information delivered through finely targeted online advertisement. It is strategically aimed at a carefully selected cross-section of people so that when it is presented to

[41]Raj, Suhasini, 'In India, Debunking Fake News and Running into the Authorities', *The New York Times*, 22 September 2022, http://tinyurl.com/fxbebsuj. Accessed on 16 February 2024.

[42]'Fake News and the Future of Journalism | Robert Hernandez | Tedxkc', YouTube, 14 September 2017, http://tinyurl.com/46rshfrs. Accessed on 20 February 2024.

> them in this manner, the information taps directly into the unique regional and cultural beliefs of its intended audience. Packaged like this, it is impossible to challenge.[43]

It is still uncertain how the menace of fake news can be fought effectively. Never before in human history have we been this helpless in the face of deception. Fake news is quickly becoming the biggest truth of our day.

---

[43]Matthan, Rahul, 'The Backfire Effect and the Menace of Fake News', *mint*, 21 February 2018, http://tinyurl.com/4s89y9z3. Accessed on 16 February 2024.

6

WHATSAPP: BLAME THE MESSENGER

This was in 2013. The campaign for the Delhi Assembly elections was in full swing, from the streets to social media, and voting was only a few days away. At that point, the Election Commission convened a meeting of all party representatives. The meeting's agenda was to demand political parties to stop campaigning on social media at 5.00 p.m.—a day and a half before voting. It was resolved at this meeting that no political party or independent candidate will campaign on Facebook, Twitter or Google Hangout during this time period. However, WhatsApp was exempt from the restriction.[1] It had been assumed that since WhatsApp was a messenger service its use was analogous to the door-to-door campaign being permitted even after the campaign had ended. Then there was the issue of not being able to easily monitor or stop the activities on WhatsApp.

This issue with WhatsApp persists even after a decade. The Election Commission and other regulatory bodies are unsure what to do with the content exchanged and shared on WhatsApp. It is essentially a messenger, and when you make groups in it, it begins to function somewhat similarly to social media. It can be used to share documents, audio, video and other multimedia items. It can also be used to make voice and video calls. It is

[1]Lal, Ankit, *India Social: How Social Media Is Leading the Charge and Changing the Country*, Hachette India, 2017.

additionally connected to the united payments interface (UPI) now. Further, WhatsApp's broadcast feature allows you to transmit messages or media to multiple contacts at once. It is already utilized for business and e-commerce. WhatsApp messages are encrypted. Even the corporation that runs WhatsApp cannot read the messages sent and received on it. Anyone can transmit any message, and if it goes viral it is difficult to determine where it originated.

By the time the Election Commission met in 2013, WhatsApp had grown in popularity in a metropolis like Delhi, at least among smartphone users. The BJP had organized worker groups on WhatsApp. The AAP had formed a team to train its members on how to use WhatsApp for political purposes. Ankit Lal talks about this strategy, saying:

> A small team gathered in a rented apartment in Kaushambi. Tasks were divided among the team members for Facebook, WhatsApp and coverage of live events. The content and graphics team was also expanded and more volunteers were roped in. The WhatsApp team was given the responsibility of visiting every constituency and training volunteers on its use. They were to teach volunteers to create groups, broadcast information and how to use the medium to spread positive news about the party and counter rumours.[2]

Although it was initially intended for party workers' coordination, it was quickly utilized to connect voters with them and deliver election campaign messages directly to the voters. The AAP set up billboards all across Delhi with their phone number and instructions on how to reach them via WhatsApp.

---

[2]Ibid.

A METEORIC RISE

In the Indian market, WhatsApp swiftly surpassed text messaging and email. In reality, during India's rapid communication revolution, WhatsApp suddenly appeared in the hands of people who had never had access to text messages or email before. When they first obtained an Android phone, a large proportion of smartphone users had to set up their first email account. To use the phone, one had to sign up with Google, and the mail account was also created along with it. However, for many, there was no need to utilize it when they had WhatsApp installed on their smartphone.

Amber Sinha, a lawyer interested in technology and the Internet, offers another explanation for how WhatsApp's popularity in India increased so quickly:

> Indian users are in the habit of consuming information in non-textual formats. WhatsApp forwards in the form of image and video files have emerged as one of the key modes of dissemination of information and news... The videos were often circulated in parts of the country where people had limited literacy and relied primarily on images or video content received on messaging apps.[3]

In a short time, India has become the world's largest WhatsApp market.[4] Today, there is almost no smartphone in the country that does not have this app. According to some estimates, there were around 535.8 million monthly active WhatsApp users in the country by 2023.[5] If we calculate it using the country's population

---

[3]Sinha, Amber, *The Networked Public: How Social Media Is Changing Democracy*, Rupa Publications, 2019.

[4]Shewale, Rohit, 'Whatsapp Statistics in 2024 (User Demographics & Revenue)', *demandsage*, 16 January 2024, http://tinyurl.com/3y864dac. Accessed on 13 February 2024.

[5]Ibid.

data, it means that approximately 38 per cent of the country's population uses it.[6]

WHATSAPP GROUPS

WhatsApp's group feature is the most used and abused. On this platform, it is extremely simple to start a group, and anyone can be added to the group. A group can have a maximum of 1,024 members. There is no official data on how many WhatsApp groups are currently operational in the country, but it is speculated that the number might be in the millions. We can comprehend how much WhatsApp has infiltrated our lives by using the example of a young man working in a media firm in Noida, UP, whom I met during a reporting assignment.

His family consists of five individuals, each of whom has a smartphone. They have a WhatsApp group where they discuss who has to do what and what they will have for dinner. Then there are two groups with his extended family: one from his father's side and one from his mother's side. These groups were formed so that family members could stay in touch. Aside from wishing them a 'Happy Birthday' and congratulating them, many other forms of messages were also being exchanged. One group consists of buddies from his school, while the other consists of friends from college. There is also a group of pals from his neighbourhood, and through this his phone number has reached the group formed by the Resident Welfare Society of his housing society. He is also a member of the group formed by his caste's adherents, in which his caste is continually glorified. He also has two office groups. The first is the official group formed by the office administration, while the second is formed by co-workers.

---

[6]Roy, Esha, and Anuradha Mascarhenas, 'India's Population 142.8 Crore in 2023, Crosses China's: UN Population Report', *The Indian Express*, 20 April 2023, http://tinyurl.com/mt864bn8. Accessed on 13 February 2024.

During the day, the office provides lunch; he is also in the group formed by the contractor that provides lunch, where the day's lunch menu arrives at 11.00 a.m. There is also a group of riders on the chartered bus that he takes to work where the information is shared on why the bus was delayed on a particular day. And, certainly, one group deserves a special mention. His name is also on the voters' list, and BJP's Panna Pramukh from his area set up a group in his neighbourhood, through which he receives all campaigning messages from the BJP. There is concern that in the near future, workers from the Congress, Samajwadi Party and BSP might also enlist him in their groups.

People in other countries might be bothered by being in so many different groups. Particularly, by being in a political party's groups where there is nothing but propaganda and fake news. Many people avoid joining such groups. However, this is not the situation in India. Shivam Shankar Singh's experience explains it quite well. He says:

> While travelling through villages on election work, first in Tripura and then in Madhya Pradesh, I realized that most voters believed that being added to a political WhatsApp group gave them access to some kind of insider information. Instead of being irritated by the messages, they read them with gusto, in the belief that they were receiving information from a credible source... The feeling was that they were receiving information that few others were aware of. They then repeated the same information in their everyday conversations with pride, shutting up people in political debates based on information that they had received over WhatsApp.[7]

There is another important aspect that technology and social media scholar Danah Boyd pointed out very rightly: 'In a networked culture, there is also power in being the person

[7]Personal interview with Shivam Shankar Singh

spreading the content.'[8] Political parties form many different types of groups. First, there are those groups designed for coordination among party members. These are mostly used for organizational purposes. These groups mainly negotiate where to conduct a meeting, where to display posters, where to say what and how to answer what. They also serve as a conduit for communication between party officials and workers. Parties, in a sense, build their own alternative information ecosystem through these groups.

Second, there are those groups that connect party workers with voters. There are various varieties of such groups, each with its own approach. Many groups are open to people of different backgrounds, but the majority consist of people belonging to a specific class, community or caste. The booth in charge of different parties, organizes a group including people responsible for getting votes cast. Many times, groups are created based on people's ideologies and interests. Previously, these groups were established using random phone numbers; currently, data analytics is used. The groups formed in this manner are more focussed and targeted.

Since its launch, WhatsApp has been at the centre of Indian politics. According to Shivam Shankar Singh, political parties created around 9,000–10,000 WhatsApp groups of workers before the 2014 general election. Among these, he believes, the BJP was first, followed by the AAP.[9] It was not possible to spread further at the time since smartphones had not yet reached a large proportion of the general public. However, this situation began to change gradually. The BJP also made great use of it in the subsequent Assembly elections. The BJP IT Cell Chief Amit Malviya told *The Economic Times* at that time: 'The upcoming elections will be

---

[8]Gillaud, Hubert, 'What Is Implied by Living in a World of Flow', *truthout*, 24 January 2010, http://tinyurl.com/5bcvvctn. Accessed on 16 February 2024.
[9]Personal Interview with Shivam Shankar Singh

fought on the mobile phone... In a way, you could say it would be WhatsApp elections.'[10]

Shivam Shankar Singh describes the effect of all this, saying:

> The BJP built a massive network of over 20,000 WhatsApp groups in just the state of Karnataka before the state went to polls in May 2018, and the party has built equally large networks in many states that have gone to polls since 2014. This means that the party has the capacity to send messages to crores of people instantly through the lakhs of WhatsApp groups it has access to across the country. This is where the BJP vastly outperforms its opposition.[11]

During the recent Assembly elections in many states in 2023, WhatsApp groups became the primary campaign tool. For example, it was reported that the Madhya Pradesh BJP organized around 42,000 WhatsApp groups among the 64,000 booths to communicate the party's election message.[12] In Rajasthan, the BJP planned to build 55,000 WhatsApp groups for electoral goals.[13] The Congress, on the other hand, claimed to have formed over 2,000 WhatsApp groups in each district.[14] What I observed while

---

[10]Narayanan, Dinesh, and Venkat Ananth, 'How the Mobile Phone Is Shaping to Be BJP's Most Important Weapon in Elections', *The Economic Times*, 23 August 2018, http://tinyurl.com/y3b5ebtb. Accessed on 16 February 2024.

[11]Singh, Shivam Shankar, *How to Win an Indian Election*, Penguin Random House, 2019.

[12]Madhukalya, Amrita, '42K Whatsapp Groups, 40L Booth-Level Workers: How BJP Won MP Assembly Polls', *Deccan Herald*, 4 December 2023, http://tinyurl.com/zc4yk72y. Accessed on 16 February 2024.

[13]Singh, Prakash Narayan, 'Rajasthan Election 2023: 55 Thousand Whatsapp Groups Will Attack Congress', *Opinion Class.*, 27 February 2023, http://tinyurl.com/4umyuhm5. Accessed on 16 February 2024.

[14]Singh, Ramendra, 'Madhya Pradesh Poll Battleground Shifts from Rallies & Posters to Posts & Shares on Social Media', *The Times of India*, 9 October 2023, http://tinyurl.com/59tazpsp. Accessed on 16 February 2024.

field reporting was that aside from that, there are groups founded by members of the parties that are not affiliated with the parties. It could be a group of individuals attending a certain temple, a group of morning walkers in a park or a group of residents from a local resident welfare association. In these gatherings, the party's propaganda is steadily pushed, and based on the reactions and engagement of the members, it is determined who supports the party and who does not. Because they are all in the group, their phone numbers are easily accessible. All of these groups are bombarded with political advertisements and misinformation, which is frequently generated at the organized level.

WHATSAPP UNIVERSITY

WhatsApp has made it possible for political parties to influence people's perceptions on a large scale. The process of spreading false information that began on social media was not only widened but also amplified via WhatsApp. This knowledge, produced in professional factories to change perceptions, has altered the political outlook of the people very quickly and on a vast scale. Many topics, ranging from history and geography to science, are presented to the public in such a way that they readily accept it. They don't even notice anything wrong because the information merely confirms their notions, even if these preconceptions appear to be unfounded to people with expertise. For example, suppose you receive a WhatsApp message informing you that the UNESCO has declared India's national anthem to be the best in the world. Since you like your national anthem, even if you have never heard the national anthem of any other country in the world, you believe your national anthem is the finest and you accept it as truth. Despite the fact that the UNESCO does not make such pronouncements by vying for national anthems from all over the world.[15]

We have explored how social media corporations' algorithms generate echo chambers for users. The same thing occurs in WhatsApp, but because there is no algorithm, users can readily be included in an echo chamber or become a member of it. WhatsApp amplifies people's biases and fallacies better than other social media platforms. It is quite simple to share and reshare the stuff included within it. This has become the most common source of fake news, hate speech, hoaxes and spam.

Many people make a serious note of this knowledge because they have no other source of information or understanding. They not only believe it, but they also tell others and dispute over it. Through this dialogue, fake knowledge reaches even individuals who have yet to own a smartphone. Nowadays, you'll see folks flaunting their knowledge at every turn and street corner. 'WhatsApp University' is a new phrase that has emerged as a result of this. This word is frequently used in satire, memes and stand-up comedy. It has also become a feature of political discourse, where it is used to mock someone who readily believes whatever biased propaganda reaches to them on WhatsApp.

A public interest litigation (PIL) was filed in the Kerala High Court in October 2021, when the Covid-19 vaccination campaign was in full swing across the country. It was stated in this petition that the state is forcing children to be vaccinated. The court determined that the petitioner filed this case only on the basis of information obtained through social media, with no further facts. The judge rejected the petition, saying, 'Don't go by WhatsApp University.' Through this judgment, the Court

---

[15]'Fake Alert: No, UNESCO Did Not Declare Indian National Anthem "Best in the World"', *The Times of India*, 19 August 2019, http://tinyurl.com/4vdp9wma. Accessed on 16 February 2024.

recognized the phenomenon of WhatsApp misinformation.[16]

VIOLENCE

There have been numerous reports of WhatsApp being used to disseminate rumours about gangs of child lifters and kidney sellers. In several parts of the country, this has resulted in the lynching of sadhus-sanyasis, beggars and even middle-class families.[17] In 2018, a mob of over 3,000 people slaughtered five labourers in Maharashtra's Dhule district only because they were suspected of stealing children.[18] There are so many of these situations that several books could be written about them.

The London School of Economics' department of media and communication conducted an in-depth study on the violence caused by WhatsApp in 2018. It concluded:

> The messages that act as a trigger are produced and disseminated in a systematic manner; they fall into clear genres; and are targeted to produce affective states in recipients that make entire communities more prone to agree to, participate in, or view violence against particular targets as legitimate.[19]

---

[16]Varghese, Hannah M., '"Don't Go by Whatsapp University": Kerala High Court Dismisses PIL Alleging Forced Vaccination of Children', *LiveLaw*, 6 May 2022, http://tinyurl.com/53jrhjke. Accessed on 16 February 2024.

[17]Vij, Shivam, 'Opinion| Rumors on Whatsapp Are Leading to Deaths in India. The Messaging Service Must Act.', *The Washington Post*, 19 June 2018, http://tinyurl.com/mpbrf234. Accessed on 16 February 2024.

[18]PTI, 'Maharashtra: Five "Child Lifters" Lynched in Dhule', *The Times of India*, 1 July 2018, http://tinyurl.com/4faewnwv. Accessed on 16 February 2024.

[19]Banaji, Shakuntala, et al., 'Whatsapp Vigilantes: An Exploration of Citizen Reception and Circulation of Whatsapp Misinformation Linked to Mob Violence in India', *LSE Research Online*, 2019, http://tinyurl.com/y7ebmwaz. Accessed on 20 February 2024.

Apart from that, WhatsApp has become a cause of political violence in various parts of the country. The police station attack during the Nuh riot in Rajasthan was planned on a WhatsApp group. Recently, WhatsApp was used in Manipur's political violence for everything from spreading rumours to targeting people.[20] When this type of violence occurs, governments normally do only one thing: they shut off the Internet service. All of this occurs so frequently in our country that India has risen to the top of the list of countries[21] that frequently suspend Internet services. As a result, India has been dubbed the 'Internet Shutdown Capital'[22] in numerous reports. But as we have seen from experience this has not been able to curb the menace.

NO END IN SIGHT

Most social media platforms provide a way to address offensive or misleading content. Users can report content they find offensive, and it may be removed upon review if it violates community guidelines. While this method is effective in handling organized dissemination of fake news, it remains controversial and is often misused. Instances have been observed where a dissenter, or someone critical of those in power, has had their profile suspended due to mass complaints, often orchestrated by political parties.

Moreover, on most social media platforms, there is an opportunity for users to point out inaccuracies in the comments.

---

[20]Singh, Vijaita, 'Manipur Officials Told to Quit Social Media Groups', *The Hindu*, 13 August 2023, http://tinyurl.com/mpbwkcs9. Accessed on 16 February 2024.

[21]Ellis-Peterson, Hannah, and Aakash Hassan, '"A Tool of Political Control": How India Became the World Leader in Internet Blackouts', *The Guardian*, 25 September 2023, http://tinyurl.com/536bbw94. Accessed on 16 February 2024.

[22]Kaskar, Zeeshan, 'India Remains Internet Shutdown Capital of the World for Fifth Year Running: Report', *The Wire*, 23 February 2023, http://tinyurl.com/369tterk. Accessed on 16 February 2024.

Although there is an option to disable comments on one's post, individuals can still share misinformation and emphasize its misleading nature to their friends. However, on WhatsApp, these messages are typically sent individually, making the spread of fake news easier.

The disruption caused in society by WhatsApp fake news, violent episodes and lynchings, among other things, put pressure on Facebook (now Meta), the corporation that owns this platform. Previously, the corporation appeared to be taking steps to combat fake news on Facebook and Instagram, but it completely ignored the issue regarding WhatsApp. The Ministry of Electronics and Information Technology filed a letter to WhatsApp about this in mid-2018. The department's minister, Ravi Shankar Prasad, also asked WhatsApp to develop a technology solution to combat fake news.[23] Earlier, WhatsApp stated that it will step up its efforts to combat fake news in India. WhatsApp said in a blog post on 20 July that it was eliminating the 'Quick Share' button that shows next to each message in order to curb the spread of fake news. It was also agreed that no communication could be forwarded in more than five chats at the same time.[24]

The issue of misinformation on WhatsApp is complicated. Its roots are in various things, from societal attitudes to political practises; such an issue cannot be remedied through technological means alone. That is why the crisis is far from ending. This problem has grown exponentially since then. And this issue has almost vanished from public discourse.

We have observed that fake news busters do not have much

---

[23]'Fix Fake Message Problem or Face Action, Ravi Shankar Prasad Tells Whatsapp', *The Economic Times*, 22 August 2018, http://tinyurl.com/yase5hnb. Accessed on 16 February 2024.

[24]PTI, 'Whatsapp Will Now Limit Forwards to 5 Recipients Globally in a Bid to Fight Fake News', *Business Today*, 21 January 2019, http://tinyurl.com/2et26thv. Accessed on 16 February 2024.

success on social media, but in the case of WhatsApp, this success is almost non-existent. Misinformation on WhatsApp is delivered in the form of messages and is not publicly visible, as it is on social media. Fake news busters can only receive such communications if they are members of the group to which the message was delivered or if someone passes it on to them. Then it is hard to determine how far this disinformation has spread, making it even more difficult for the truth to reach all those corners.

Another major issue with WhatsApp is data harvesting. Any member of any group can obtain the phone numbers of every other member. A large database can be established by collecting many similar numbers for a city or state from various groups. In India, mobile phone numbers are linked to Aadhaar numbers. Theoretically, if Aadhaar data is obtained, it is simple to determine who is engaged in which group. Their names and addresses can also be obtained. The manner in which previous reports of Aadhaar data leaks emerged indicates that the danger is quite real.[25] It can also be determined which person is affiliated with what kind of thinking and how active he is. This can result in a detailed map of a person's contacts and activities. WhatsApp is capable of providing the most significant service of political data analytics.

WhatsApp is the most important weapon in any political party's arsenal, and it is the most important battleground in today's politics. As a result, it is nearly guaranteed that no stone will be left unturned on this front. We must remember what Ankit Lal, the man who has been in charge of AAP's social media initiatives for a long time, said—'We wrestle on Twitter. The battle is on Facebook. The war is on WhatsApp.'[26]

---

[25]Sapkale, Yogesh, 'Aadhaar Data Breach Largest in the World, Says WEF's Global Risk Report and Avast', *MoneyLife*, 19 February 2019, http://tinyurl.com/e6hr7tue. Accessed on 20 February 2024.

[26]Goel, Vindu, 'In India, Facebook's Whatsapp Plays Central Role in Elections', *The New York Times*, 14 May 2018, http://tinyurl.com/yeyjkuzw. Accessed on 16 February 2024.

7

CYBER LUMPENS AND ARMIES OF TROLLS

There was a period when the strongmen and lumpens of one party would not allow individuals from the opposing party to speak or campaign. Their stage was destroyed, and their posters and banners were ripped. Through trolling, the same task has begun to take place on online platforms at a more sophisticated and wider scale. It can be even crueller at times. This is a new manifestation that we refer to as 'poll-related violence'.

Trolling refers to purposely abusive behaviour on any online platform that is intended to harm someone. This emotionally fractures the other person and drives them to react. Trolling content is designed in such a way that anyone who sees it becomes tremendously upset and scrambles to respond. In general, the goal of such behaviour is to silence opposing voices, as well as to generate a sense of scorn or opposition to them in society. Trolling is also frequently used to interrupt political discourse. The goal is to keep people distracted from real issues and enmeshed in emotional things.

This happens throughout the world, but the organized and purposeful way it began in India has transformed the entire political landscape. Its most vulnerable targets are active and successful women in public life. Trolls feel that by making vulgar and lewd comments about them or assassinating characters, they can silence them. Not only women leaders, but also journalists, actresses, lawyers, social workers, etc., are targeted.

NO ONE IS SPARED

When Narendra Modi's government appointed Sushma Swaraj as foreign minister in 2014, she was the most senior and popular female politician in the country. *The Wall Street Journal* even referred to her as the country's 'best-loved official'. [1] After taking charge of the foreign ministry, she decided to engage with the public in addition to her official duties. She used Twitter as a vehicle for this, and began addressing people's concerns connected to her department. She assisted many people, particularly with visa and passport issues. Despite the fact that India–Pakistan relations were deteriorating, she arranged visas for Pakistani children who wished to come to India for treatment and surgical procedures.[2]

On another instance, a woman took to social media alleging harassment by the passport office staff in Lucknow. She accused that she was harassed by one official because of her marriage to a Muslim man. The woman sought justice from Swaraj on Twitter.[3] The Union Minister took action against the accused.[4] What followed was abominable.

Swaraj was trolled heavily on Twitter. She was subjected to a slew of nasty and sexist insults.[5] Some expressed their solidarity

---

[1]Varadarajan, Tunku, 'India's Best-Loved Politician', *The Wall Street Journal*, 24 July 2017, http://tinyurl.com/5vw23b4. Accessed on 16 February 2024.

[2]Jha, Vaibhav, 'Sushma Swaraj Throws Lifeline to Lahore Toddler for Heart Surgery in Noida', *Hindustan Times*, 11 June 2017, http://tinyurl.com/mt6y9dvy. Accessed on 16 February 2024.

[3]'Lucknow Woman Alleges Harassment by Passport Office Staff for Marrying a Muslim, Seeks Sushma Swaraj's Help', *The Indian Express*, 20 June 2018, http://tinyurl.com/4z839af7. Accessed on 16 February 2024.

[4]PTI, 'Sushma Swaraj Takes on Trolls, Retweets Messages She Received after Lucknow Passport Row', *India Today*, 25 June 2018, http://tinyurl.com/2mweb6sf. Accessed on 16 February 2024.

[5]'Sushma Swaraj Is the Latest Victim of Right-Wing Trolling', *The Wire*, 25 June 2018, http://tinyurl.com/yc3vuc6x. Accessed on 16 February 2024.

with the passport official and further remarked that she had received a kidney from a Muslim man and that was the reason she took action.[6]

India's Foreign Minister is considered among the most influential people in the country. However, she was helpless in the face of online abuse. Prime Minister Narendra Modi and his Cabinet members made no public statements in support of one of their senior colleagues. The lone exception was Rajnath Singh, the then minister for home affairs, who condemned the trolling. However, we expect the Minister for Home Affairs to go beyond censure and take action.[7] Sushma Swaraj was giving to the world an example of how social media can be used to serve people, but we quickly saw what the fate of such intentions could be.

A piece in *Hindustan Times* provides additional details.[8] According to the report, 41 BJP MPs, including Cabinet officials, followed people who were trolling the External Affairs Minister on Twitter. There were eight trolls who were being followed by Prime Minister Narendra Modi's official account. While this does not imply that those individuals agreed with anything the troller posted, nevertheless, we can deduce the status of those trollers from this. Isn't this indicative of our new politics?

A few years before Sushma Swaraj's trolling, in 2015, PM Narendra Modi had hosted a meeting with his social media supporters at his official house on Race Course Road in New Delhi. Around 150 social media supporters attended this event. Among them were some Twitter users who were infamous for

---

[6]Swaraj had had kidney transplantation some years ago; Ibid.

[7]Chaturvedi, Rakesh Mohan, 'Rajnath Singh Lone BJP Voice in Government to Support Sushma Swaraj', *The Economic Times*, 3 July 2018, http://tinyurl.com/mrysykfk. Accessed on 16 February 2024.

[8]'41 BJP Lawmakers Follow Twitter Users Who "Trolled" Sushma Swaraj', *Hindustan Times*, 26 June 2018, http://tinyurl.com/2ktrdrv5. Accessed on 16 February 2024.

bashing women and making rude and nasty comments about them.[9]

EVEN HOME MINISTER UNSAFE

Let us now discuss Rajnath Singh, the then home minister, who had criticized the trolling of his Cabinet colleagues. On social media, he was labelled a detractor. People started calling him a '*Ninda Mama*' (an uncle who only finds faults). Later, after a terrorist attack on Amarnath pilgrims, Rajnath Singh hailed some Kashmiris for condemning the attack and speaking out against it. Following this, numerous trolls began speaking out against the country's Home Minister. One troll wondered if he was a 'real Thakur', while another wondered if he had ever attended an RSS Shakha. And, like at the time of Sushma Swaraj's trolling, none of his colleagues were spotted supporting him. If even the Home Minister is vulnerable to online trolling, we can deduce the entire ecosystem of trolling that exists on social media.[10]

Swati Chaturvedi, a journalist, has authored a book about trolling called *I am a Troll: Inside the Secret World of the BJP's Digital Army*. The majority of this book is based on her personal experiences. She then met the folks that trolled her and attempted to comprehend their reasoning.

Sadhavi Khosla's story is the most crucial element of her book. Sadhvi, who was working in the US, returned to India with her children and, drawn by the chants of change, joined the BJP's IT cell. Allegedly, her job was to troll the who's who

---

[9]'Twitter Trolls among #SUPER150 Invited by PM Modi', *the quint*, 6 July 2015, http://tinyurl.com/4m4ud4yu. Accessed on 16 February 2024.

[10]Kohli, Karnika, 'Colleagues Keep away as Right Wing Trolls Target Rajnath Singh', *The Wire*, 12 July 2017, http://tinyurl.com/yd6pu73a. Accessed on 16 February 2024.

of opposing viewpoints. She claimed she immediately realized she was wrong when trolling Aamir Khan, Rajdeep Sardesai and Barkha Dutt, among others.[11] She found herself unable to troll people she considered her heroes so she left the task. Khosla's confession demonstrates the professionalism with which this trolling operation is carried out. It is a separate story that the BJP afterwards claimed Khosla never worked for them.[12]

'INDIA'S MOST TROLLED WOMAN'

Any discussion on trolling in India would be incomplete without discussing Barkha Dutt. She has been dubbed 'India's most trolled woman'.[13] There have not been as many vulgar comments directed towards anyone else as have been directed at her. Every fourth trolling revealed that Barkha Dutt is married to a specific individual. The person whose name was usually taken was either a foreigner or a Muslim. And in many cases, no one with that name even existed. They not only called her a traitor but also threatened her with rape and murder. Even her mother, a well-known and respected journalist, was subjected to obscene remarks. Her phone number was made public on social media, and the trolling that had previously occurred on online platforms began to reach her phone directly.[14] Many journalists, including

---

[11]'BJP Ex-it Chief Denies Orchestrating Online Campaign against Aamir Khan', *Hindustan Times*, 28 December 2016, http://tinyurl.com/2xfphnay. Accessed on 16 February 2024.

[12]Chaturvedi, Swati, *I Am a Troll: Inside the Secret World of the Bjp's Digital Army*, Juggernaut, 2016.

[13]Pasricha, Japleen, '10 Media Cases That Show Online Harassment Is Not an Isolated Issue', *Feminism in India*, 6 December 2016, http://tinyurl.com/2zhnzanu. Accessed on 16 February 2024.

[14]Ramani, Priya, 'Why Everybody Loves to Hate Barkha Dutt', *mint*, 23 April 2016, http://tinyurl.com/3c9mdfyp. Accessed on 16 February 2024.

Ravish Kumar, have fallen victim to this.[15] Even those who were seen with Dutt were humiliated. BJP MP Meenakshi Lekhi was also trolled when she shared the stage with the journalist in one location.

Even though trolling and mudslinging couldn't stop Barkha Dutt from carrying on with her job, what she wrote about it in her column in *Hindustan Times* displays her grief nevertheless:

> Frankly, now, trolling has become part of my daily life. I don't even notice it anymore; that's how dangerously inured I have become to the gross innuendo and violent and sexually explicit abuse that is heaped on so many women. But this is so wrong. And our silence—my silence, my numbed weary acceptance of it or even my defiant engagement with it—is a disservice to all our women. Because in the end, trolling is a modern-day weapon of patriarchs; an attempt to control, intimidate and eventually silence women, all of us who think for ourselves.[16]

This type of trolling, however, was not limited to Barkha Dutt. This long list includes names like Sagarika Ghose, Rana Ayyub, Kavita Krishnan, Teesta Setalvad, Meena Kandasamy and Kiran Rao.[17] It is also said that all women in public and on social media have experienced trolling at some point. Many have said that they receive no assistance from the police administration in such a situation. The administration frequently states that if women

---

[15]'NDTV's Ravish Kumar Says Death Threats Have Increased', *The Hindu*, 25 May 2018, http://tinyurl.com/vka39td5. Accessed on 16 February 2024.

[16]Dutt, Barkha, 'Let's Talk about Trolls | Online Abuse a Weapon to Silence Women: Barkha Dutt', *Hindustan Times*, 12 May 2017, http://tinyurl.com/tpccuzuv. Accessed on 16 February 2024.

[17]Pasricha, Japleen, '10 Media Cases That Show Online Harassment Is Not an Isolated Issue', *Feminism in India*, 6 December 2016, http://tinyurl.com/2zhnzanu. Accessed on 16 February 2024.

want to avoid such trolling, they ought not to create a social media account in their own name. That implies that the onus is ultimately on the women who are the victims of trolling.[18]

BEYOND SOCIAL MEDIA

This story of women being trolled is not limited to social media. In 2021, it was revealed that an app called Sulli Deals[19] had been posted on the *GitHub* website. 'Sulli' is a pejorative epithet used to describe Muslim women. *GitHub* is a cloud-based software development platform. The Sulli Deals app had pictures of notable Muslim women in the country up for auction. Pages like 'Sulli Deals of the Day' were formed as a result of this. When the complaint was received, Delhi Police blocked the app, but a few days later, another similar app called Bulli Bai appeared.[20]

THE RISE OF CANCEL CULTURE

Not only Muslim women but also Muslim men have been frequent targets of trolling. Many celebrities, including Aamir Khan, Saif Ali Khan and Shah Rukh Khan are still being trolled; particularly, if one of their movies is soon to be released. Even now, men who are outspoken and think differently from the prevailing narrative are heavily trolled. This is true also in the case of journalists who dare to question the establishment.

---

[18]Ibid.

[19]'"Sulli Deals" Muslim Women "Auction" App Creator Arrested in Indore: Police', *NDTV*, 9 January 2022, http://tinyurl.com/jnxp5kst. Accessed on 16 February 2024.

[20]Salim, Mariya, '"Bulli Bai", "Sulli Deals": On Being Put up for "Auction" as an Indian Muslim Woman', *The Wire*, 16 January 2022, http://tinyurl.com/vvaxt46s. Accessed on 16 February 2024.

Efforts are also being made to mark many of them as Muslims.

Cancel culture is another trolling-related practise. In this, they attempt to fully reject a person by trolling him or her. There is also a call for a 'boycott'. Aamir Khan's story perfectly exemplifies this phenomenon.

Aamir Khan faced backlash for his views on rising intolerance in India. Trolls targeted him for alleged 'love jihad' after his marriages to Hindu women. The situation worsened when he expressed concerns about the country's atmosphere of fear, leading to calls to boycott him. Aamir's film, *Lal Singh Chaddha*, faced protests and calls for a boycott resulting in a box-office flop. However, the film later found success on Netflix, highlighting the real-world impact of trolling beyond virtual hatred. Shah Rukh Khan's film *Pathan* faced a similar boycott attempt but emerged as the highest-grossing film of 2023, challenging the perceived influence of trolls on film success. The incidents showcased the troll army's power in influencing public opinion and causing real-world consequences.

This isn't only about liking and disliking movie stars or films. It also has multiple political sides. In her book, *The Three Khans and the Emergence of New India*, famous journalist Kaveree Bamzai offers another perspective. She describes how Salman Khan, Aamir Khan and Shah Rukh Khan became the most popular heroes at one time and how their heroism was lost. She says:

> By articulating ideas from political meritocracy to menstrual hygiene, by implementing decisions long pledged by the BJP, Prime Minister Modi has colonised the Indian imagination, leaving very little space for other icons. His relentless publicity machine has ensured that he, more than any other public figure, now helps India understand itself. This was what the Three Khans had once done, in their own ways, helping Indians navigate from tradition to modernity, as they

> themselves moved from the callowness of youthful romances to bigger themes. India had seen itself in the three of them.[21]

It was required to ruin these movie stars in order to elevate Narendra Modi to the height of heroism.

There are numerous examples that make it appear that only those from the BJP and the Right wing engage in trolling. However, this is not totally correct. To comprehend this, we must watch on YouTube, two speeches given by PM Narendra Modi in August 2023. The first was a speech he delivered in reply to the Opposition's no-confidence motion in Parliament. On 15 August, he delivered his second speech from the ramparts of the Red Fort. Both of these speeches were streamed live on YouTube. On both occasions, the PM's address was being delivered as he was being trolled in the comment section. The case is the same with the PM's or any BJP leader's tweets. They are trolled in the majority of the replies.

There are numerous similar examples. For instance, in May 2016, while campaigning in Thiruvananthapuram, Kerala, PM Modi compared Kerala to Somalia in terms of infant mortality among scheduled tribes. As a result, he was viciously attacked on Twitter.[22] In December 2019, Modi was ridiculed on Twitter for wearing eyeglasses worth ₹1.6 lakh while observing the solar eclipse.[23] In March 2020, Modi was brutally trolled for announcing that he was leaving social media.[24]

---

[21]Bamzai, Kaveree, *The Three Khans: And the Emergence of New India*, Westland Non-fiction, 2021.

[22]'PM Modi Gets Trolled on Twitter for Comparing Kerala to Somalia', *BangaloreMirror*, 11 May 2016, http://tinyurl.com/p5dwba9n. Accessed on 16 February 2024.

[23]'PM Modi Gets Trolled on Twitter for Wearing Sunglasses Worth ₹1.6 Lakh', *HWEnglish*, 26 December 2019, http://tinyurl.com/2af3wr27. Accessed on 16 February 2024.

[24]Chatterjee, Pramit, 'PM Narendra Modi Gets Brutally Trolled for Announcing He's Leaving Social Media', *Mashable India*, 3 March 2020, http://tinyurl.com/ysen4yyw. Accessed on 16 February 2024.

The deployment of evil tactics in politics isn't a one time thing, but rather a gradual and stealthy integration into the political practices, potentially capable of causing lasting harm. Over time, these methods spread, leaving everyone feeling pressured to resort to them. We've seen this happen with muscle power, black money and now it's playing out with fake news and trolls.

8

THE MAKING OF A PAPPU

Politics is a game of perception. Building and breaking images is how one plays this game for the win. Insulting, maligning and mocking one's political opponent are all allowed, and there is nothing new about these dirty tricks in electoral politics. But there was a time when there was more to politics, when issues of import hadn't taken a backseat yet. However, in the last one and a half decade, politics has increasingly become only about smearing leaders and candidates. And the most alarming change in the last decade is that all of this dirty work gets done in an organized and large-scale manner. An army of keyboard activists are now being trained to carry out this operation. The process of ruining someone's image can now be done intelligently, thanks to social media.

During the Bharat Jodo Yatra, Rahul Gandhi said that the BJP had spent millions of rupees to tarnish his reputation. This project is said to have cost a vast amount of money. It is unclear how Rahul got the information regarding the money and to what extent it is true, but given how this campaign has been running continuously everywhere, it is evident that such a thing cannot be done without a certain kind of investment.

A TALE OF TWO LEADERS

The tale of Indian politics over the last decade and a half is as much about the growth of the BJP and Narendra Modi becoming PM as it is about the biggest Opposition party leader being converted into a *pappu*. In terms of marketing, just two things have been done throughout this time period: the branding of Narendra Modi and the negative branding of Rahul Gandhi. It took just as much effort to make one a hero as it did to make the other a laughingstock. Traditional media as well as social media have been utilized against him. He was the target of the most memes and cartoons in Indian politics. The most fake information is spread against him. So far, he is the country's biggest victim of trolling. He was the focal character in a majority of jokes throughout the last decade. At times, it appears that Indian society has devoted its entire sense of humour to mocking only one person.

The brutal smear campaign against Rahul Gandhi began in 2013. At that time, it was evident that Manmohan Singh was in his last innings. The UPA government's position was steadily weakening for a variety of reasons. Rahul Gandhi seemed like Congress's next best hope at the time. As the government's credibility kept going down, many people in the country were looking up to Narendra Modi for a new start. The BJP, led by Narendra Modi, was making a big effort to criticize Rahul and damage his reputation. They used various strategies and were determined to make sure that no aspect was left untouched in their negative branding of Rahul Gandhi.

Pappu is not a terrible word; it is the most prevalent nickname in North India. Children are often named pappu. But when the same word is used to refer to an adult, the connotation of the meaning changes. It then refers to a person who has grown physically but has a childish mind. It is frequently used in this context to mean foolish.

The word pappu had been present in the popular imagination of Indians. During the mid-2000s, a Cadbury chocolate commercial became highly popular on television media, with the tagline '*Pappu pass ho gaya* (Pappu has passed)'.[1] It became so popular that a film with the same title was made afterwards.[2] The line 'pappu can't dance'[3] was used again in a song. When the national capital's elections were held in 2008, the Delhi Election Commission created an advertisement campaign to encourage people to vote, with the tagline 'Pappu can't vote'. Using Pappu to mean 'foolish young man' became popular during those times.

By the time this smear campaign started, it had been a decade since Rahul had been involved in politics, and he had also risen through the ranks to become the Congress vice-president. However, slowly a narrative started to emerge that he had no great accomplishments to his name up to that point. Opponents of the Congress have long claimed that dynasties from the Nehru–Indira Gandhi line are entitled to the highest seat in politics simply because of their family ancestry.

Some have said that Rahul Gandhi had a chance to firm his footing in 2009, as his party won more seats than the previous election. He could have gotten credit for this triumph if he had played a significant impact in that election. Or he could have played a larger part in the government formed following the elections, but he did not do so. On top of that, he made a number of statements that definitely did not help his case. One of his famous quotes from the time was 'power is poison'.[4] The hashtag #powerispoison began to trend on Twitter. During an election rally in Bangalore, Narendra Modi, the then CM of Gujarat, said:

---

[1]Magan, Srishti, 'From "Kuch Khaas" to "Pappu Paas Ho Gaya", Here's Revisiting Cadbury's Iconic Ads', *SW*, 17 September 2021, http://tinyurl.com/yfhdwuj5. Accessed on 16 February 2024.

[2]Dutta, Prabhash K., 'How Rahul Gandhi Became "Pappu" of Politics', *India Today*, 23 July 2018, http://tinyurl.com/37scjt9p. Accessed on 16 February 2024.

[3]Ibid.

[4]PTI, 'My Mother Cried, She Understands Power Is Poison: Rahul Gandhi's Emotive Speech', *India Today*, 21 January 2013, http://tinyurl.com/3u79fenv. Accessed on 16 February 2024.

'Mother says "power is poison" and son (Rahul) comes calling in Karnataka seeking power to the party.'[5]

This statement is still used to demonstrate Rahul's ineptitude in politics. However, what Rahul had said had an entirely different context. It was said at his maiden address as party vice president at All India Congress Committee (AICC) session in January 2013 in Jaipur. In his emotive speech he had said, 'My mother came to my room and cried... because she understands that power is poison.'[6]

Rahul spoke with Arnab Goswami of *Times Now*[7] news channel shortly before the elections. It was a huge blunder on the part of the Congress or Rahul's media team to have him give his first interview to a hostile anchor, while there were plenty more options available. Arnab Goswami was known for his confrontational demeanour, which effectively silenced others. Arnab did the same thing this time. On the other hand, while interviewing Narendra Modi a few days later, Arnab was calm, polite and restrained.[8] However, Rahul's media management made a blunder, which added a lot of spice to him being attacked on social media.

Although Rahul was part of the party, and one of Congress's top prime ministerial contenders, the Grand Old Party did very little investment into building Rahul's image. Rahul himself also seemed not so bothered about creating an image that would appeal to the voters. As a result, a huge percentage of the populace may

---

[5]'In Bangalore, Modi Flays Rahul Gandhi', *The Tribune*, 29 April 2013, http://tinyurl.com/252u4jz5. Accessed on 16 February 2024.

[6]PTI, 'My Mother Cried, She Understands Power Is Poison: Rahul Gandhi's Emotive Speech', *India Today*, 21 January 2013, http://tinyurl.com/3u79fenv. Accessed on 16 February 2024.

[7]'Frankly Speaking With Rahul Gandhi - Full Interview | Arnab Goswami Exclusive Interview', YouTube, 28 January 2014, http://tinyurl.com/2mpmwwxz. Accessed on 20 February 2024.

[8]'Frankly Speaking with Narendra Modi - Full Interview', YouTube, 9 May 2014, http://tinyurl.com/3x2k2v9s. Accessed on 20 February 2024.

have felt that they did not know what he stood for in politics. What was his position, and what did he seek? By then, he had become the party's president and was keen on talking about intra-party democracy. Beyond that, no one understood what his worldview was or what he thought about the country. This made BJP's job easier. They created a perception of Rahul as someone lacking vision. In the eye of the public, his only qualification was that he was Rajiv Gandhi's son. In speeches, BJP leaders like Narendra Modi referred to him as *Rajkumar* (Prince). The perception of him was of a political dynast with no credential—he was seen as someone who was worth nothing.

TRENDING MALICE

Once this trend began, every speech delivered by Rahul, every comment he made and every action he took was examined under a microscope. Flaws were being discovered in them. Where faults were not discovered, they were manufactured. Before the sixteenth Lok Sabha elections in 2014, Rahul had delivered a speech in Delhi at the Confederation of India Industries (CII) convention. He had brought along a prepared speech, but at the last minute he set it aside and spoke impromptu.[9] *The Tribune*'s editor-in-chief, Raj Chengappa, was there when Rahul delivered this speech. After that event, he penned an article expressing his admiration for the speech.[10] Rahul, he added, had finally stood up. However, by the time this article was published, the hashtag #PappuCII had trended on Twitter. Hashtags with the name Pappu were becoming increasingly common.

---

[9]'Rahul Opens up to India, Talks of Change Spells Out His Vision before India Inc: Focus on Inclusive Growth', *The Tribune*, 5 April 2013, http://tinyurl.com/vbr86wxd. Accessed on 16 February 2024.

[10]'Rahul Gandhi and the Importance of Being Earnest', *The Tribune*, 7 April 2013, http://tinyurl.com/2jsczfmu. Accessed on 16 February 2024.

The hashtag #AccordingToRahulGandhi became a popular trend on Twitter following Rahul's remarks about Coca Cola's origins.[11] Netizens used it to mock and ridicule his mistake. One example was a photo that was shared of Shammi Kapoor with a comment claiming that #AccordingToRahulGandhi Shammi Kapoor was the founder of Yahoo (refering to his iconic song 'Chahe Mujhe Koi Junglee Kahe' where he sings 'yahoo' in jest).[12]

Afterwards, several hashtags began to be used concurrently on every single Rahul speech. Rahul visited Somnath temple with party leader Ahmed Patel during the 2017 Gujarat elections. Then, word got out that Rahul had proclaimed himself non-Hindu in the temple register. On Twitter, many hashtags such as #RahulHinduVivad and #RahulHinduorCatholic were created to ridicule him.[13] There was an attempt to demonstrate that Rahul is a Catholic rather than a Hindu. At 9.00 p.m., 29 November 2017, *Times Now* organized a prime-time debate on this topic in which another hashtag, #RagaSomnathSelfGoal, was mentioned. The pointless conflicts on social media were suddenly dictating the narrative for television news. It was never known who made such entries in the temple register until now. It was neither Rahul's nor Ahmed Patel's handwriting.[14]

Looking at the real issues of politics, all of this was a pointless debate. But by then, politics had reached a point where whether someone was a Hindu or not had become quite important. While

---

[11]'Twitter Rewrites History #Accordingtorahulgandhi after He Claims Coca Cola Founder Sold Shikanji', *Scroll.in*, 12 June 2018, http://tinyurl.com/49hwz8uu. Accessed on 16 February 2024.

[12]@gogiinc, X (formerly Twitter), 14 June 2018, 1.56 p.m., http://tinyurl.com/ycxe4uc4. Accessed on 20 February 2024.

[13]Sinha, Pratik, Sumaiya Shaikh and Arjun Sidharath (eds), *India Misinformed: The True Story*, Harper Collins Publishers India, 2019.

[14]'Rahul's Name in Somnath Temple's Non-hindu List: Why Is That News?', *the quint*, 29 November 2017, http://tinyurl.com/mr23nd8c. Accessed on 16 February 2024.

efforts were made to prove that Jawaharlal Nehru, Indira Gandhi and Rajiv Gandhi were Muslims, those mocking Rahul branded him a Catholic as well. The photo of Rahul donning a skull cap had been posted thousands of times by that point, trying to prove something else as well. Two images were posted for comparison, one of Narendra Modi wearing a tilak and the other of Rahul wearing a skull cap. The photo was captioned, 'One fights for truth, the other advocates terrorism.'[15]

Another photo was also shared during this time. In this image, Rahul is seen writing something on a piece of paper while seated with Congress leaders, including former PM Manmohan Singh, as Jyotiraditya Scindia stands nearby. Aurangzeb's portrait was displayed on the wall behind where Rahul sat in this photograph. The caption said, in Hindi, 'Which nationalist's portrait have these patriots hung?'[16] When the photograph was examined, it was discovered that the original contained Mahatma Gandhi's portrait on the wall, which had been removed and Aurangzeb's picture was recreated using Photoshop. There are several examples of such fake news, and it is impossible to list them all.

The reality behind many of these pieces of fake news has also been revealed. We've seen before that the truth never becomes as viral as fake news. However, when fake news against someone exceeds certain bounds, they begin to appear ineffectual. The same thing happened in the case of Rahul Gandhi. The communal type of fake news has lost its impact over time. Such things could not seriously affect his reputation. However, there was one instance in which Rahul's image was severely harmed, and he was unable to make a quick recovery.

---

[15]'Fake Alert: Old Video of Rahul Gandhi's Dargah Visit Used to Suggest He's a Muslim', *The Times of India*, 19 December 2018, http://tinyurl.com/6nyrvkjk. Accessed on 16 February 2024.

[16]Patel, Jignesh, 'Image of Rahul Gandhi with Portrait of Aurangzeb in Background Viral on Social Media', *alt news*, 17 July 2018, http://tinyurl.com/mw5n65k2. Accessed on 16 February 2024.

For a long time, efforts were made to portray Rahul as a good-for-nothing, immature and foolish individual. This had an effect on the public, and many people formed this image of him in their minds. Such unfavourable branding became highly associated with him. Every time, an attempt was made to determine whether or not he was capable of running the government or even his party. Some BJP officials used to poke fun at him on any possible occasion. Furthermore, Amit Shah stated at an event in Mayurbhanj that Narendra Modi had worked for the previous 20 years for 18 hours a day, but Rahul Gandhi used to travel abroad every two months, and his mother was unaware about where he had gone.[17] In his rallies, the PM has solely mentioned 'Naamdar' and 'Kaamdar' to compare himself to Rahul. The 'Naamdar' or the man who has a name and fame because of his clan was Rahul, while Modi was a 'Kaamdar' who is famous only for his work.[18]

The BJP may be credited with crafting this image of Rahul, but all anti-Congress parties capitalized on it, even those who did not support the BJP. The AAP in Delhi, for example, and TMC in West Bengal. The TMC leader, Mamata Banerjee, spoke of Rahul, saying, 'Rahul Gandhi is just a kid.'[19] When 23 big Congress leaders established the G-23 group in 2020 and declared rebellion against the party's high command, their problem was also Rahul's image. They believed that if his negative image continued, the party's chances of winning would come to an end.

---

[17]PTI, 'Narendra Modi Works 18 Hours a Day While Rahul Gandhi Takes Leave Every 2 Months: Amit Shah', *CNBC News 18*, 27 April 2018, http://tinyurl.com/34e6na3a. Accessed on 16 February 2024.

[18]PTI, '"Kamdar" in Fight against "Naamdar" This Election: PM Modi in Rajasthan', *The Times of India*, 28 November 2018, http://tinyurl.com/3bxfd546. Accessed on 16 February 2024.

[19]'"Rahul Gandhi Is Just a Kid", Says West Bengal CM Mamata Banerjee', YouTube, 28 March 2019, http://tinyurl.com/6pubsa5d. Accessed on 20 February 2024.

TRYING TO REDEEM RaGa

In the face of incessant smear campaigns, the Congress decided to play one of the oldest tricks in the book, which worked to some extent. Congress launched Bharat Jodo Yatra with Rahul at the helm. *Padyatras*, or long marches, have been crucial in Indian politics since Mahatma Gandhi's Dandi March in 1930. In 1930, the 387-km excursion was in protest of the British government's decision to tax salt. This provided a new dimension to the country's protest politics. Following it, many political marches were conducted in the country on a regular basis.[20]

In 1983, Chandra Shekhar, often known as the Young Turk, travelled from Kanyakumari to Delhi. This journey solidified his position as a national leader. He later became the PM for a brief period.[21] Sunil Dutt had performed a padyatra from Bombay (now Mumbai) to Amritsar at a time when the Punjab situation was causing concern throughout the country. This journey elevated him from a movie star to a full-fledged politician.[22] Similarly, in Andhra Pradesh, Rajasekhara Reddy used his padyatra to bring the marginalized Congress back into the mainstream, and he then became the state's CM.[23]

No one knew what the Bharat Jodo Yatra would lead to when Rahul planned it. Many members of the Congress did not take it seriously. Opponents questioned Rahul's ability to complete the march from Kanyakumari to Kashmir. It was only natural to doubt a young man whose entire image had been built around being from a comfort-loving dynast of a famous clan. Rahul

---

[20]Sinha, Sarojini, *A Pinch of Salt Rocks an Empire*, Children's Book Trust, 1985.

[21]*Chandra Shekhar*, http://tinyurl.com/48e8brmj. Accessed on 20 February 2024.

[22]'Chandra Shekhar Comes to the End of His 4-Month Padayatra from Kanyakumari to Delhi', *India Today*, 6 June 2014, http://tinyurl.com/y7rr4rkt. Accessed on 16 February 2024.

[23]Undavalli Arun Kumar, *Padayatra 9th April 15th June, 2003 My Diary YS Rajasekhara Reddy Praja Easthampton*, Sahithi Books, 2010.

was involving more individuals from NGOs for this Yatra than members from his own party, and as a result, his politics were not on anyone's radar. People were wondering what kind of outcome this march would produce. K.C. Venugopal, the party's leader, responded, 'We are demolishing the factory of lies constructed by the BJP about Rahul Gandhi over the past 10 years. Now the villagers of India are seeing for themselves who Rahul Gandhi is.'[24]

Bharat Jodo Yatra was the name given to this expedition. This journey, which began on 7 September 2022, in Kanyakumari, lasted 150 days and covered a distance of 4,080 km. It was terribly hot and humid when this Yatra began in Kanyakumari. When it came to an end in Kashmir, there was continual snowfall.[25]

Rahul regularly walked the entire journey. During his journey, he came across a variety of people, had conversations with them and also had lunch and dinner with them. He also held one or two press conferences per week. He demonstrated patience in answering all of the vexing issues. Following this, many beliefs were automatically debunked. No one can now suggest that he is a man who can do nothing apart from living a nice life. The phrase 'he is from a dynasty' has no meaning now. He was walking to stay in the Yatra and was not running away.

Meanwhile, the fake news factory's production continued unabated. The Bharat Jodo Yatra included a one-day break day in between. The first day of rest was spent in Thrissur, Kerala. The banned Islamist organization The Popular Front of India (PFI) called a *bandh* on this day. Rahul was claimed to have

---

[24]'From "Pappu" to Popular: Can the Bharat Jodo Yatra Remake Rahul Gandhi's Image?', *The India Fix*, 10 October 2022,
http://tinyurl.com/2a3ecfs9. Accessed on 20 February 2024.

[25]Zargar, Safwat, 'Heavy Snowfall, Sparse Crowd, Mixed Feelings: Bharat Jodo Yatra Comes to an End in Srinagar', *Scroll.in*, 31 January 2023,
http://tinyurl.com/3dnmm9pb. Accessed on 16 February 2024.

halted his march in favour of the bandh.[26] During the Bharat Jodo Yatra, a BJP leader claimed that a girl was raising 'Pakistan Zindabad' slogans at the rally. The Congress threatened to file charges against that leader. In another instance, a photo was used to try to explain how people were brought in buses to join the march. It was later discovered that all of the buses belonged to Jai Gurudev sect members travelling to Mathura. One time, a glass of wine was photoshopped onto a photo of Rahul eating at a *dhaba* and uploaded on social media.[27]

But none of this mattered anymore. Every day, Rahul was providing more real news than the fake news manufacturing system could produce. Throughout the journey, Rahul did not shave. His beard had begun to run by the time the padyatra arrived in Delhi. Some BJP leaders compared him to former Iraqi President Saddam Hussein.[28] However, it had a positive impact on the people. Prahlad Kakkar, who has extensive expertise in the advertising industry, gave a noteworthy opinion, saying, 'The beard has given him a certain degree of seriousness. He has arrived as a man, he is no longer Indira Gandhi's grandson, neither Rajiv Gandhi's son. He is now Rahul Gandhi, the man. That is a very critical change in how people perceive him today.'[29]

The opinions on the political success of the Bharat Jodo Yatra

---

[26]Beri, Vasudha, 'Bharat Jodo Yatra Halted in Support of PFI Bandh in Kerala? No, Viral Claim Is Not True', *newschecker*, 23 September 2022, http://tinyurl.com/3k76vp6z. Accessed on 16 February 2024.

[27]Kujur, Anupa, 'Fact-Check: Viral Photograph of Rahul Gandhi Drinking Alcohol during Bharat Jodo Yatra Is Morphed', *Deccan Herald*, 11 January 2023, http://tinyurl.com/mwvyy2j5. Accessed on 16 February 2024.

[28]'Looks Like Saddam Hussein: Assam CM Mocks Rahul Gandhi over Bharat Jodo Yatra Look, Cong Hits Back', *India Today*, 23 November 2022, http://tinyurl.com/4rye2j9f. Accessed on 16 February 2024.

[29]Sharma, Chirali, 'Is Rahul Gandhi Changing His Image with Bharat Jodo Yatra 1 &2?', *EDTimes*, 5 January 2024, http://tinyurl.com/yxya6w5c. Accessed on 20 February 2024.

are divided.[30] One critique is that the Congress was unable to prepare a follow-up programme to engage the public support shown around the country during this Yatra. But there is no doubt that Rahul has been freed from the image of being a pappu through this march, even if it meant walking thousands of kilometres over the course of five months. The most important thing is that he put an end to the internal party rebellion.

Rahul recognized the significance of such efforts. He later paid a visit to a motor maintenance shop in Delhi's Karol Bagh and had a lengthy conversation with the shop owner.[31] When tomato prices skyrocketed, he made a visit to Azadpur vegetable market. He also went to the home of the vegetable seller, who was unable to buy tomatoes one day owing to a lack of money and was forced to stop work. A few days later, Rahul was seen walking through the streets of Ladakh[32] and then in a carpentry workshop at Kirti Nagar, Delhi[33].

It's also true that if his branding had been done correctly at the beginning, he might not have become the subject of ridicule to this extent. We can also learn from the example of Narendra Modi. Modi's opponents did not leave any stone unturned in their campaign against him. He was referred to as 'Gappu' and 'Feku'.[34]

---

[30]The later stages of the Bharat Jodo Yatra, particularly after Delhi, received extensive media coverage.

[31]Gupta, Aman, 'Rahul Gandhi Meets Bike Mechanics in Delhi's Karol Bagh, Congress Says "Bharat Jodo Yatra Continues.."', *mint*, 28 June 2023, http://tinyurl.com/3cpde3r2. Accessed on 16 February 2024.

[32]PTI, 'Rahul Gandhi's Ladakh Trip Is Continuation of "Bharat Jodo Yatra", Says Congress', *The Hindu*, 22 August 2023, http://tinyurl.com/khu7ner4. Accessed on 16 February 2024.

[33]'Rahul Gandhi's Another Reach-Out Exercise. This Time at Delhi's Kirti Nagar Furniture Market', *Hindustan Times*, 28 September 2023, http://tinyurl.com/ywya7bdv. Accessed on 16 February 2024.

[34]Kapoor, Mugdha, 'A Brief Story of How Modi Went from #Feku to #Gappu in a Year!', *India Times*, 25 May 2015, http://tinyurl.com/h4sw8a6x. Accessed

Rahul himself referred to Modi's government as a '*suit-boot ki sarkar*', and the slogan '*chowkidar chor hai*' was used against him. However, no such endeavour was successful beyond a certain point.

The number of errors Rahul makes in his speeches and comments might probably be lesser than Modi's. The PM's opponents were never able to gain a political advantage. Instead of simply trying to damage PM Narendra Modi's reputation through slogans, the Congress may have inadvertently given him a new rallying cry. By adopting the title 'Chowkidar Narendra Modi' on his Twitter account, the PM has turned the tables on his critics and potentially resonated with voters who see him as a strong protector of the nation. Other BJP leaders have also embraced the 'Chowkidar' label, creating a sense of unity and purpose within the party. Modi's personal brand has grown so strong that any negative branding cannot penetrate it.

---

on 20 February 2024.

PART THREE

THE INDUSTRY

9

BUSINESS OF ELECTIONS

Congress leader Jag Pravesh Chandra, the grand old man of Delhi politics, had authored a short book titled *How to Win Elections* sometime in the latter half of the twentieth century. Central News Agency published this 128-page book.[1] The tricks and tips shared in the book are from a time when election campaigning meant going door to door, pasting posters, giving leaflets, travelling around the city yelling slogans on loudspeakers, encouraging people to vote and having street corner gatherings and big rallies.

Chandra describes how elections should be organized in the book. He writes about how to determine the areas that needs the most attention while campaigning, how a candidate should interact with voters and also how they should treat workers and volunteers of the party. Workers, he claims, are the backbone of any electoral campaign.

The only significant change since Chandra published this book is that the backbone has mostly been replaced. Workers and volunteers continue to labour tirelessly and enthusiastically to help their candidate or leader win, but their position is no longer as important as it was once. It is true that the workers still play a very significant role in the party's campaigning strategies, but at the same time the scope of their function has reduced. There are various reasons for that, like the massive increase in India's

---

[1]Pravesh Chandra, Jag, *How to Win Elections*, Central News Agency.

population. Consider the UP Lok Sabha constituency of Unnao. It is not the country's largest Lok Sabha constituency, either in terms of size or number of voters. Even then, in the most recent general election, approximately 22 lakh voters were there. It is impossible for any politician to campaign door to door and meet all the voters.

So, the politicians have had to resort to other ways to reach their voters like social media, exploiting Big Data and other options. To accomplish these, the politicians have enlisted the help of professional election managers. However, many have pointed out that the use of these managers has done much harm to politics. The grassroots workers were dedicated to the philosophy of the party or the leader. But that is not necessarily the case with these professionals. If an individual is handling the election campaign for one party's leader today, they can handle the campaign for another party's leader tomorrow. They are not committed to any political ideology. As any other professional service, the principal objective of these institutions is their fees.

Almost everyone has acknowledged that the new era's aspirations cannot be realized using conventional approaches. As a result, the usage of political consultants during elections is steadily expanding. It is being used not just by national and regional parties, but also by many candidates in their constituencies. However, Indian politics did not take this path suddenly. It took many decades.

THE ARUN TRIO

Following Indira Gandhi's humiliating defeat in the 1977 elections, the environment in the 1980 elections was once again favourable to her. Sanjay Gandhi, her son, was particularly involved in this election. Arun Nehru, a member of the Nehru family, was one of the members of Sanjay's team. He was the president of Jenson & Nicholson (J&N), a paint production company. J&N's advertising was handled by Rediffusion, an agency owned by his friend Arun Nanda. This prepared the way for Rediffusion to be introduced to the Congress. Sanjay also wanted to give the election campaign a modern look. Thus, it was decided that Rediffusion would prepare a presentation and show it to Indira. She is believed to have sat through the 2-hour and 45-minute presentation at 1, Safdarjung Road with bated breath, but she was not convinced that such an advertising campaign could reach every voter. Elections were approaching, and there was no time for further discussions, therefore Rediffusion's attempts came to a halt here.[2] However the Congress won the elections and Indira returned to power.

Sanjay tragically died in a plane crash the same year. Soon after, Rajiv Gandhi entered politics. He eventually included his best friend Arun Singh in his team. Previously, Prince Arun Singh of the Kapurthala royal family was in charge of the British multinational Reckitt & Colman. This company's advertising campaign was likewise handled by Rediffusion. Another point to mention is that Rajiv, Arun Singh and Arun Nanda all went to school together. By then, Arun Nehru had already become an MP after winning the Rae Bareli by-election. This time, Rajiv and the three Aruns persuaded Indira to give Rediffusion a chance. Everyone recognized that as the population of the middle class in our country was growing at that point, there would be a need for professional content for election campaigns sooner or later.[3]

Despite the fact that the general elections were still three years away, the Congress and Rediffusion signed an agreement in 1982.[4] Thus began the professional age in Indian politics. It was

---

[2]Kumar, Aloke, 'My Brush with Indira Gandhi', *This & That*, 8 November 2012, http://tinyurl.com/f482xptc. Accessed on 18 February 2024.

[3]Bikhchandani, Raghav, '"Rajiv Gandhi Ka Ailan/Nahi Banega Khalistan": When Ad Agency Helped Congress Score Big 1984 Win', *ThePrint*, 20 March 2022, http://tinyurl.com/5b2hduj7. Accessed on 18 February 2024.

[4]Dhar Sharma, Amogh, 'Concertina Wires and the Crocodile: The General

assumed that much planning would be required for a Himalayan endeavour as elections. This was the same Congress that was thought to be aware of everything people desired and had workers in every town, street and corner, who came out running with the flag as soon as elections came around. Since then, the Congress has been known for unbeatable electoral slogans. Slogans like 'Jai-Jawan, Jai Kisan', 'Garibi Hatao' and '*Na jat par-na paat par, Indira Ji ki baat par, mohar lagegi haath par* (Neither on caste, nor on social rank, only on Indira ji's words, will stamp on the hand)' were always changing the election narrative.[5]

THE CONGRESS BANKS ON FEAR

This was a period of great turmoil in many parts of the country. Terrorism in Assam and Punjab remained a source of concern for New Delhi. When terrorism erupted in Punjab, Indira launched Operation Blue Star in 1984 to destroy the terrorists gathered in Amritsar's Golden Temple. She was assassinated a few months later by two of her bodyguards. Following her terrible murder, anti-Sikh riots erupted in Delhi and other parts of the country, and India's political narrative was altered.

There was anxiety and dread among the populace. When the general elections were held a few months later, Rediffusion's advertising campaign reflected the fear and apprehension. In these black-and-white ad campaigns, every approach for attracting people's attention was tried. Some had crocodiles, some had barbed wires and still others had hawthorns as symbols, with slogans like, 'Will the country's border finally be moved to your

---

Elections of 1984 and the Rise of Political Marketing in India', *LSE*, 13 March 2023, http://tinyurl.com/446tdxbp. Accessed on 18 February 2024.

[5]'"न जात पर-न पात पर, इंदिरा जी की बात पर, मुहर लगेगी हाथ पर?"- लेफ्ट के जवाब में कांग्रेस', *Dainik Bhaskar*, http://tinyurl.com/42tbxkmp. Accessed on 18 February 2024.

doorstep?', 'Will another war be the last war in the life of free India?' and 'Will the groceries list in the future include acid bulbs, iron rods, daggers?'

Many elements in the advertising confirmed people's fears. 'Give Unity a Hand' was the slogan.[6] These ads were heavily criticized by opponents. It was said that the Congress used terror tactics to sway voters. However, the scale, artwork and sophistication of these advertisements were significantly superior to those of the Opposition parties. Because the country's circumstances were unusual, the election was also peculiar. It was difficult to discern if those at the polling booths were voting or paying tribute to Indira on election day. The Congress made history when it won 404 seats.[7] The outcome may have been the same if the Rediffusion advertising campaign had not been undertaken in that situation. But the truth is that the advertising had made an impression.

When the next elections were held five years later, the political climate in the country had shifted once again. Rajiv, formerly known as 'Mr Clean', had faced many allegations against him. A number of scams had been exposed including the Bofors controversy.[8] Aside from that, a big segment of the middle class was upset with the Congress's approach of Muslim appeasement in the Shah Bano case.[9] Vishwanath Pratap Singh, a former senior Cabinet colleague, had raised the rebel flag against Rajiv and Singh's popularity was

---

[6]Dhar Sharma, Amogh, 'Concertina Wires and the Crocodile: The General Elections of 1984 and the Rise of Political Marketing in India', *LSE*, 13 March 2023, http://tinyurl.com/446tdxbp. Accessed on 18 February 2024.

[7]*Statistical Report on General Elections, 1984 to the Eighth Lok Sabha, Volume I*, Election Commission of India, 1985.

[8]'What Is the Bofors Scam Case?', *The Indian Express*, 3 February 2018, http://tinyurl.com/mte3ubc9. Accessed on 18 February 2024.

[9]Gupta, Shekhar, Inderjit Badhwar and Farzand Ahmed, 'Shah Bano Judgement Renders Muslims a Troubled Community, Torn by an Internal Rift', *India Today*, 16 January 2014, http://tinyurl.com/ycxuftns. Accessed on 18 February 2024.

growing.[10] Arun Nehru and Arun Singh had abandoned Rajiv, but the third Arun—Arun Nanda—and his Rediffusion continued to campaign for him in the 1989 national elections.

Initially, the Congress considered certain alternatives. It evaluated agencies such as Clarion and Tara Sinha Associates before settling on Rediffusion.[11] Clarion then took over the BJP's election campaign then.[12] The advertising budget of the Congress for the 1984 general elections was expected to be around ₹8 crore, while during the 1989 elections, the advertising budget was estimated to be around ₹50 crore, including ₹20 crore as fee for services provided by Rediffusion.[13]

These adverts were sent around the country in newspapers, magazines and other publications. Given the uncertainty about who would win, some publications refused to accept advertisements for fear of not receiving their money if the party lost. Of course, the publications' previous experiences of not getting paid by a party that lost the election could have also played a factor. Meanwhile, the Indian Newspaper Society advised that all publishing houses seek payment in advance for such advertisements. There was a worry that if a party loses, it might not pay for the advertisements, as it had done so on many other occasions.[14]

LIGHTNING NEVER STRIKES TWICE

Rediffusion's previous ad campaign had garnered some criticism, but this time it received widespread condemnation. People

[10]Bhattacharya, Shubhabrata, 'May 1981-May 1991: The Turbulent Decade of Rajiv', *The Sunday Guardian*, 22 May 2021, http://tinyurl.com/2j7bn5rm. Accessed on 18 February 2024.

[11]S.N. Vasuki, 'Election Media: Congress(I) Ad Campaign Flops', *India Today*, 12 November 2013, http://tinyurl.com/5n6h82p8. Accessed on 18 February 2024.

[12]Ibid.

[13]Ibid.

[14]Ibid.

expected the Congress to talk about its accomplishments, but the 1984 formula was restored in 1989. They decided to stoke people's fear of unitability that the country had experienced around the time Indira was assassinated. But that was not at all the country's mood. There was no fear and apprehension in the population as there had been in previous elections, but Congress' advertisements included cartridges, broken dolls, scorpions and the tearing down of a tree. The slogan of these advertisements was 'My heart beats for India'.[15] In *The Indian Express*, a cartoonist created a series of cartoons mocking these adverts.[16]

This election was significant in one way. Although audio and video cassette technology had existed for some time, it had only recently begun to reach the public at the time of this election. Audio cassettes were so prevalent in this election that microphone and loudspeaker campaigns were almost halted. Professionally made cassettes as well as player devices and speakers were now widely used. The message could also be communicated to the public through songs and music. But the video van was the topic of discussion during this election. A video van is a vehicle equipped with a large screen that travels to every street, nook and village to display the party's video advertising material. Most parties and leaders had specifically prepared videos for this. The 1989 general elections, however, were most notable for transforming organization-based elections into media-based elections—now parties also focussed on public outreach using media.

The elections were a disaster for the Congress. They won only 197 seats, a sharp decline from the 404 from the last election.[17] Of

[15]Crosette, Barbara, 'Selling of India: Tough Ads by Congress Party', *The New York Times*, 15 November 1989, http://tinyurl.com/bdz8ufwm. Accessed on 18 February 2024.

[16]Ibid.

[17]'General (9th Lok Sabha) Election Results India', *Elections.in*, http://tinyurl.com/y8p43dwt. Accessed on 18 February 2024.

course, the atmosphere manufactured against the Congress was the primary reason for this, but what Rediffusion did was also a factor in the defeat. When the Congress triumphed in 1984, no credit was given to Rediffusion, but when it lost in 1989 it was blamed. This was and continues to be a concern for political professionals.

When advertising firms had entered the field, it was impossible for public relations firms to get left behind. The importance of media-based elections was to depict candidates in a positive and polished manner. This was the era of regional and numerous small parties. Their new leaders had no prior experience dealing with the media. Everyone now had a new platform for promotion thanks to the launch of satellite television networks and cable channels. Even many old and experienced leaders did not know how to give quick and crisp soundbites for television at the time. That's why, when public relations firms joined the electoral market in the 1990s they found plenty of work.

Perfect Relation of Delhi was one of the first organizations to enter this industry. Dilip Cherian, founder of Perfect Relation, said, 'At that time, the concept occurred to mind that if we slightly tweak the techniques, we use to persuade consumers, we may influence people in the same way. […] So that when the time comes for them to vote, they will remember what we have said.'[18]

Things began to change after the 2004 general elections. By then, the mobile phone had already made a grand entry in the country. But it was not yet time to develop a big strategy based on mobile phones. At the time, the central government was led by Atal Bihari Vajpayee. We've already discussed how the BJP used his voice to rally support at that time.

By then, the hiring of experts in elections had begun to rise at all levels. One sign of this was that the vocabulary that was previously only used in the business world was now being used in politics as well. When discussing the performance of their

[18]Personal interview

government, BJP leaders used to assert that the country's 'feel good factor' had increased during their tenure. Previously, the CII used the term 'feel good factor' in its annual business outlook report. The BJP had directly borrowed this term from them.[19]

The BJP entrusted their election campaign to the advertising agency Grey Worldwide, which was part of the Grey Global Group in New York. This corporation had risen to prominence by establishing Samsung and Hyundai in the Indian market. This agency created the slogan 'India Shining' for the BJP. This slogan quickly gained popularity among city dwellers. The BJP had also placed high hopes on this. Later, the slogan 'Abki Baari, Atal Bihari' was also used, but by that time, 'India Shining' had become synonymous with the BJP's electoral campaign.

This campaign had begun a long time ago, and it was widely anticipated that the BJP would easily win this election. The BJP's triumph was publicly demonstrated when the 'Mood of the Nation' survey was published in the 9 February 2004 issue of *India Today* magazine. On the cover was a portrait of Atal Bihari Vajpayee with the tagline 'Landslide for Atal'.[20]

In response, the Congress picked a US-based advertising agency for its campaign. When Chicago-based Leo Burnett took over the Congress election campaign, there was a lot of chatter about the BJP. The agency could only respond to 'India Shining' in one way. For each advertising, it had produced two slogans. The first was used to highlight concerns about the BJP's campaign, asking, '*Aam adami ko kya mila* (What did the common man get)?' and '*Congress ka haath, aam admi ke sath* (Congress's hand is with the common man).'[21] These slogans succeeded, and when

---

[19]Thuppil, Vivek, 'The Feel Good Factor', *Outlook*, 28 May 2004, http://tinyurl.com/zf8abuj3. Accessed on 21 February 2024.

[20]*India Today*, 9 February 2004.

[21] 'Where's the "Aam Aadmi" in the Congress Campaign?', *mint*, 24 January 2014, http://tinyurl.com/5d48s673. Accessed on 21 February 2024.

the election results came in, the Congress had become the largest party in the new Lok Sabha leaving the BJP in second place.[22]

Three important incidents in 2008 had an impact on public opinion in the country. The first was the Indo-US nuclear accord[23], for which then PM Manmohan Singh risked his government. The country's middle class overwhelmingly supported it, while many political parties, including the BJP, opposed it.[24] Then there was a huge economic recession, and many of the world's economies crumbled. It appeared that it might have a negative impact on India as well, but India dodged its effects and the growth rate did not dip below 6.5 per cent.[25] And, before the end of the year, on 26 November, there was a terrorist attack in Mumbai. This was the largest terrorist attack the country had seen. It was an injury that jolted the entire nation.[26]

The BJP saw a huge opportunity in this entire episode. It began to sniff success by portraying this government as weak as an outcome of a weak PM.[27] This time, Lal Krishna Advani was declared as BJP's prime ministerial candidate, and the BJP had already begun to refer to him as an Iron Man. The entire election campaign was supposed to revolve around him. This time around, the BJP has partnered with not one but two advertising

---

[22]M. Sundar, Jayshree, *Don't Forget 2004: Advertising Secrets of an Impossible Election Victory*, Vitasta Publishing Pvt Limited, 2022.

[23]'India, U.S. Reach Landmark Nuclear Agreement', *NBC News*, 1 March 2006, http://tinyurl.com/a7zaxwue. Accessed on 18 February 2024.

[24]*Indo-Us Nuclear Deal: Why BJP Oppose It?*, Bharatiya Janata Party, August 2008, http://tinyurl.com/2xbypca4. Accessed on 18 February 2024.

[25]Kumar, Rajiv, and Pankaj Vashisht, *The Global Economic Crisis: Impact on India and Policy Responses*, ADBI Institute, 2009, http://tinyurl.com/2ddav4us. Accessed on 18 February 2024.

[26]'15 Years of 26/11: Remembering Horrific Mumbai Attacks', *India Today*, 25 November 2023, http://tinyurl.com/4t2eyw2u. Accessed on 18 February 2024.

[27]Kumar, Devesh, 'No "Bhay" Anymore, It's "Jai Ho"', *The Economic Times*, 17 May 2009, http://tinyurl.com/jamjk3at. Accessed on 18 February 2024.

agencies: Frank Simoes and Utopia.[28] For the Ministry of Tourism, Frank Simoes launched the 'Atithi Devo Bhava' campaign, which proved highly successful. The same advertising firm began the BJP's campaign for the Madhya Pradesh Assembly elections in 2008, which the party also won.[29]

Because the entire campaign intended to revolve around Lal Krishna Advani, advertising companies conducted extensive research. Many different kinds of slogans were tested in the market. Finally, the motto '*Majboot Neta, Nirnayak Sarkar* (Strong Leader, Decisive Government)' [30] was adopted. The BJP believed that by using this slogan, it would be able to compete with Manmohan Singh's government and the Congress.

The Congress, on the other hand, relied on some of its accomplishments. It included factors like growth rate and nuclear deal to entice metropolitan voters and rural employment guarantee schemes to entice rural voters. The Congress had delegated control of its electoral campaign to two advertising firms, Crayon Advertising and JWT India.[31] The tagline was created in accordance with Congress's positioning: '*Aam adami ke barhte kadam, har kadam par Bharat buland* (The common man's growing steps, India is mighty at every step).'[32]

Looking back on the 2009 general elections, we can see that it was an election that marked the beginning of a completely professional era of election management. Many of its symptoms

---

[28]PTI, 'BJP Hires Frank Simoes, Utopia for Poll Campaign', *Business Standard*, 20 January 2013, http://tinyurl.com/e7wt3yx6. Accessed on 18 February 2024.

[29]PTI, 'BJP Hires Ad Companies for Polls', *The Economic Times*, 9 March 2009, http://tinyurl.com/45464xbe. Accessed on 18 February 2024.

[30]'BJP Empanels Frank Simoes-Tag and Utopia', *tac*, 12 March 2009, http://tinyurl.com/mwthn4by. Accessed on 18 February 2024.

[31]'Congress Hires JWT, Crayons', *campaign India*, 23 January 2009, http://tinyurl.com/eud5z376. Accessed on 18 February 2024.

[32]Shah, Kunal M., 'The Politics of Lyrics', *Times Entertainment*, 6 March 2009, http://tinyurl.com/27dyrvc2. Accessed on 18 February 2024.

were also obvious in this election. The elections were not left to the advertising agencies alone this time. Parties were starting to realize that attracting eyeballs was just as crucial as effective marketing. To ensure that the party had a prominent spot on television channels and publications, the BJP hired a number of organizations that were in the business of getting political parties prime-time slots for their ads.[33] In response, the Congress retained the services of Mindshare. This electoral game made its way to the Internet, and Google set up an online election centre[34] that displayed a variety of crucial information regarding the 2009 Lok Sabha elections to get some benefit from the election atmosphere.

The business community also became involved in order to capitalize on the environment produced by this election. Tata Tea introduced the 'Jaago Re' campaign.[35] In addition, a website called *jagore.com* was launched. The goal was to encourage first-time voters to vote. And, under this guise, efforts were undertaken to connect young voters with their brand. Simultaneously, Idea Cellular launched the 'Janata Ki Awaaz' campaign.[36] Websites like *India-Elections.com*, *Indiannumbers.com* and *Indiavoting.com* were also launched.

There is no need to go into depth on the election outcomes here. In short, people rejected the BJP's 'weak and powerful'[37] narrative, and the Congress won more seats than the previous election. Manmohan Singh once again became the PM.

---

[33]PTI, 'Political Parties Likely to Spend Rs 800 Crore on Ads', *The Economic Times*, 24 April 2009, http://tinyurl.com/pkab5wb8. Accessed on 18 February 2024.

[34]Ibid.

[35]D'Souza, Nilofer, 'Waking up to Brand Success', *Forbes India*, 21 February 2014, http://tinyurl.com/mr23k98f. Accessed on 18 February 2024.

[36]'Elections 2009: Ad Campaigns Finally Making Politics "Cool" in India', *e4m*, 9 March 2009, http://tinyurl.com/5xdjytp8. Accessed on 18 February 2024.

[37]The BJP was attempting to send a message to the people that Manmohan Singh is a weak and indecisive PM, whereas his opponent, Lal Krishna Advani, is a strong and determined leader.

At the same time as the country's general elections in 2009, Assembly elections were also held in Orissa (now Odisha). Amid the nationwide uproar and publicity surrounding the general elections, this election received very little notice in the national media. However, this was the country's first election in which a party engaged professional consulting agency for every facet of the election. Naveen Patnaik's Biju Janata Dal was the party in question. For the elections, he hired Viplav Communication Private Limited. Pallav Pandey, an IIT Kanpur graduate, was the company's promoter.[38]

Based on the strategic advice of Viplav Communication, Naveen Patnaik decided that his party would contest the polls on its own this time around, instead of forming an alliance with the BJP as it had done last time. This tactic worked, as his party got 103 of the 147 seats in the legislature.[39] In some ways, these outcomes were also a declaration of victory for election management professionals.

Surprisingly, the AAP did not hire a consultant to run its campaign in the 2013 election. Many professionals joined the party and began working as volunteers after being impressed by its ideals. Dilip Pandey, an IT professional, quit his job in Hong Kong to join the AAP. Pankaj Gupta, another software engineer, quit his job and took over the party's finances.[40] He raised funds for the party through online crowdsourcing. Psephologist Ashish Talwar[41] also joined the party. He was familiar with each ward

---

[38]V.K. Shashikumar, 'Wired for Victory, Sirji', *OPEN*, 19 June 2009, http://tinyurl.com/3fn9fnd3. Accessed on 19 February 2024.

[39]'Orissa Assembly Election Results in 2009', *Elections.in*, http://tinyurl.com/mt28st3k. Accessed on 19 February 2024.

[40]Madan, Karuna, 'Delhi Election: Meet AAP's Backroom Boys', *Gulf News India*, 11 February 2015, http://tinyurl.com/fem8ccs6. Accessed on 19 February 2024.

[41]Chopra, Ritika, and Soma Banerjee, 'The Aam Aadmi of AAP: 5 Personal Stories of Sacrifice, Triumph and Validation', *The Economic Times*, 12 December 2013, http://tinyurl.com/5xtjmpba. Accessed on 19 February 2024.

of Delhi and proved invaluable to the party. There are numerous examples of such professionals. Some people did not quit their jobs but instead began working part-time for the party.[42]

They came up with slogans together and ran social media campaigns. Surveys were done in a variety of locations, for immediate feedback. And the party's plan was created by combining all these elements. The party decided to issue a distinct manifesto for each constituency. As a result of all this, when the elections were held, the newly established party emerged as the second largest party[43] and was given the opportunity to form a government. The government did not endure long, but that is another story.

WHO IS PRASHANT KISHOR?

The 2014 general elections were held immediately following the Delhi Assembly elections. Election managers were used at the national level for the first time in this election. Although it is widely assumed that the first major election in which professionals were fully utilized was the 2013 Delhi Assembly elections, the truth is that at a time when this election had not even begun and the AAP had not even been formed, Gujarat's Narendra Modi had begun preparations to contest the 2014 general elections.

Citizens for Accountable Governance or CAG, was founded a year before the 2014 general elections.[44] It was founded by Prashant Kishor, who was the chief of the UN mission in Chad

---

[42]Lal, Ankit, *India Social: How Social Media Is Leading the Charge and Changing the Country*, Hachette India, 2017.

[43]'Delhi Assembly (Vidhan Sabha) Elections Results 2013', *Elections.in*, http://tinyurl.com/57s5m2k5. Accessed on 19 February 2024.

[44]Venugopal, Vasudha, 'Narendra Modi's Citizens for Accountable Governance (Cag): Will It Be Disbanded or Play Bigger Role?', *The Economic Times*, 15 May 2014, http://tinyurl.com/2s3b233m. Accessed on 19 February 2024.

in his earlier avatar[45] before coming to Gandhi Nagar to assist then Gujarat CM Narendra Modi. This organization's name was a brilliant ruse. The CAG was a popular abbreviation in newspapers and on television back then, but it stood for Comptroller and Auditor General.[46] This organization, led by Vinod Rai at the time, claimed to have exposed various financial scams perpetrated by the central government. The entire narrative of Manmohan Singh government's corruption began here. Prashant Kishor's CAG attracted high-paying professionals from the corporate sphere. If we look at this organization's LinkedIn page, we can see that these things are stated with great pleasure:

> CAG was initiated by a group of spirited professionals and has been expanding to include young people from diverse and prestigious educational and professional profiles. Members of CAG belong to institutes like IITs, IIMs, Stanford University, Cornell University etc. and have served organizations like McKinsey, All India Radio, J.P. Morgan, The Indian Express, Boston Consulting Group etc.[47]

Prashant Kishor's CAG's main task was to prepare Narendra Modi's election plan for 2014, which he performed quite well. Across the country, youth conferences were held. There were programmes such as '*Chai par charcha* (a conversation over tea)'.[48]

---

[45] Venugopal, Vasudha, 'Meet Prashant Kishor, the Man Who Shaped Narendra Modi and Nitish Kumar Campaigns Now in Demand Globally', *The Economic Times*, 28 October 2015, http://tinyurl.com/55prbx5j. Accessed on 19 February 2024.

[46] 'Cagey: What's in an Acronym?', *The Economist*, 10 February 2014, http://tinyurl.com/4r4pd54t. Accessed on 19 February 2024.

[47] 'Citizens for Accountable Governance', LinkedIn, http://tinyurl.com/5jhxv6kd. Accessed on 21 February 2024.

[48] 'BJP's Answer to Tea Vendor Jibe: A "Chai Par Charcha" Campaign to Pitch Narendra Modi', *NDTV*, 4 February 2014, http://tinyurl.com/mvf9ppwh. Accessed on 19 February 2024.

Its work included field surveys, feedback and public relations. Along with this, the organization recommended candidates for different constituencies. This organization also used to advise on how to generate buzz and what certain leaders should say in their speeches. It also pioneered the usage of 3D holograms in Indian elections for the first time.

A 3D hologram is a three-dimensional projection that may be viewed without the use of any specialized equipment such as glasses. The image can be viewed from any angle so that when the viewer moves around the screen, the object appears to move and shift realistically. Voters around India were now able to experience Narendra Modi's speech virtually live. This organization was responsible for the popular tagline: '*Achhe din aane waale hain* (Good days are on their way).' Prashant Kishor's work for the party's whole election management through CAG in this general election quickly established industry standards. He continued to do the same after leaving the BJP. Meanwhile, Prashant became the poster boy of India's political consultancy industry.

While the BJP was organizing this work, the Congress was still following the old pattern. The main difference this time was that the Congress had also been involved on social media, but not as intensely as the BJP. To counter the BJP's 'Chai pe charcha', Rahul began holding Google Hangouts meetings with workers.[49] However, the party relied primarily on the old practice of rallies and advertisements.

This time, advertising was delegated to three agencies: Taproot, JWT India and Dentsu India.[50] The goal was to portray

---

[49]PTI, 'Rahul Gandhi Interacts with Party Workers on Google Hangout', *India Today*, 15 March 2014, http://tinyurl.com/nhaudm7d. Accessed on 19 February 2024.

[50]Mitra Dasgupta, Pritha, 'Congress Picks Dentsu, Taproot & Jwt for Poll Ad Campaign', *The Economic Times*, 8 October 2013, http://tinyurl.com/5n8dyyyy. Accessed on 19 February 2024.

Rahul as a young and vibrant leader. '*Har Hath Shakti, Har Hath Tarakki* (Power for all, Progress for all)'[51] was the campaign's key slogan. 'Aam Aadmi' was a key part of the slogan that had helped the Congress win its last two elections. However, Delhi's AAP prevented the Congress from using this label.[52] In addition, a 'Face of the Congress' campaign was launched.[53] The BJP also used slogans like '*Har Hath Lollipop* (Lollipop for all)'[54] to mock the Congress' slogan.

When the results came in, the Congress was crushed. In its whole history, it had never had so few seats. Following the defeat, the Congress leaders blamed the setback on the Japanese advertising agency Dentsu India. This company allegedly collected ₹600 crore[55] but did not handle the assignment properly. This defeat of Congress was viewed as more than just an electoral defeat. In some ways, this was also the loss of the old election management system at the hands of the new growing professional system.

The upcoming election became even more crucial as a result of technological advancements. Between 2016 and 2019, India's society and politics were radically transformed. This was a time when digital consumption in the country was skyrocketing. It

---

[51]Mathew, Liz, and Anuja, 'Congress Launches 2014 Election Campaign', *mint*, 25 January 2014, http://tinyurl.com/7mhc3346. Accessed on 19 February 2024.

[52]Naqshbandi, Aurangzeb, 'AAP Effect: Cong Drops "Aam Aadmi" Slogan', *Hindustan Times*, 26 January 2014, http://tinyurl.com/5969jks9. Accessed on 19 February 2024.

[53]Shri Dahiya, Medha, 'Face of Congress Ad Faces Social Media Fury', *Hindustan Times*, 1 February 2014, http://tinyurl.com/s6h5zm44. Accessed on 19 February 2024.

[54]'YouTube Spoof on Rahul Gandhi Ad Goes Viral, BJP Hand Suspected', *India Today*, 5 March 2014, http://tinyurl.com/3faybfzv. Accessed on 19 February 2024.

[55]Sarkar, John, 'Congress Blames Ad Agency for Lok Sabha Polls Debacle', *The Times of India*, 20 May 2014, http://tinyurl.com/yrj8r72v. Accessed on 19 February 2024.

only takes two figures to grasp this. In 2014, 65.3 million people used the Internet in the country. By 2019, that figure had risen to 581.5 million.[56] Cheap gadgets and data put smartphones, the Internet and social media in the hands of a vast portion of the country's population. More than half the country's voters had Internet access, and for those who did not, political messages could be delivered by party workers who were a major element of the digital campaign. Meanwhile, according to a Google study, non-metropolitan urban areas account for more than half of all searches in India.[57] This technological advancement had altered the grammar of political mobilization not just at the national but also at the local levels.

The BJP was in power at the time, and things had changed for it on several fronts. The party's strategizing and campaigning efforts were handed over to Prashant Kishor's organization CAG in the 2014 general elections. However, Prashant and his CAG parted with the BJP after the election. The CAG became a business corporation, and its name was changed to Indian Political Action Committee, or I-PAC.[58] This firm also ran campaigns for a variety of political parties in several states.

When CAG was working on the 2014 elections, an NGO called Sarvani Foundation was founded to empower women. Initially, this NGO also assisted acid attack victims. Later on, not much was spoken about it. After some time, word arrived that the name and structure of this NGO had been modified and that it had been transformed into a firm called Association of Billion Minds[59],

[56]Mehta, Nalin, 'Digital Politics in India's 2019 General Elections', *engageEPW*, 27 December 2019, http://tinyurl.com/2skkdycr. Accessed on 19 February 2024.

[57]Ibid.

[58]It was a not-for-profit organization

[59]Bansal, Samarth, 'How Modi, Shah Turned a Women's NGO into a Secret Election Propaganda Machine', *Huffpost*, 4 April 2019, http://tinyurl.com/3hkmss6k. Accessed on 19 February 2024.

abbreviated as ABM. Himanshu was one of the key members of the CAG team, along with Prashant Kishor. He became a promoter for ABM. Despite the fact that ABM was an independent firm, it served as the BJP's in-house political consultant for a long period after 2014. It was crucial in the 2019 elections. The BJP used the services of another firm in this election. Jervis Technology and Strategy Consulting Private Limited was the name of this company, which was also an offshoot of CAG. This company's sole client was the BJP, for whom it worked in numerous elections.[60] The BJP commissioned Piyush Pandey of Olive & Mother to create advertisements for the 2019 general elections.

Many factors were working against the BJP at the time, particularly on the economic front. The unemployment rate was at its peak, there was a liquidity crisis in the market and there was a recession. The business community had yet to fully recover from the effects of demonetization and GST. All of these factors were entirely neglected in the BJP campaign. There was mention of India's unity in relation to Pulwama and surgical strikes, and PM Modi was maintained at the centre of every campaign.[61]

The Congress, on the other hand, used the services of a professional for the first time. Matilde Giglio, who researched 'Youth Engagement in Politics through Social Media' at the London School of Economics, was assigned this task. By 2019, Rahul had become the party's president, with all the responsibilities. He brought up the topic of corruption in the Rafale deal and coined the slogan 'Chowkidar Chor Hai', which was aimed squarely at Narendra Modi. Even before the Congress could capitalize on this slogan, the BJP had prepared a rebuttal, as mentioned earlier. Every BJP leader began

---

[60]Mehrotra, Karishma, 'Its Team Drawn from Modi's 2014 Campaign, Mumbai Firm Works on BJP's 2019 Run', *The Indian Express*, 2 May 2019, http://tinyurl.com/528u8myy. Accessed on 19 February 2024.

[61]Sen, Ronojoy, 'Indian Elections 2019: Why the BJP Won Big', *Isas*, 1 June 2019, http://tinyurl.com/5bhwb9j6. Accessed on 19 February 2024.

writing Chowkidar as a prefix to his or her name and launched a '*Main bhi chowkidar* (I am also a Chowkidar)' campaign.[62]

This is hardly the only instance where Congress' actions have backfired. Matilde Giglio's services were also ineffective for the party. Matilde returned from India and posted a blog on the London School of Economics' website, revealing that she had no prior knowledge of Indian elections or conditions. As a result, the Congress lost terribly again this time. Rahul resigned as party president, accepting responsibility.[63]

The Congress's flaws were once again revealed. Its campaign machinery proved far weaker than the BJP's. An example will help us comprehend. Jarvis established 161 call centres for the BJP in which roughly 15,000 callers were deployed for the 2019 general elections[64], whereas the Congress established 20 call centres.

NEXT GENERATION POLITICIANS?

Political consultants are being recruited right into a party itself. Consider the case of Amrish Tyagi. He was a member of the Cambridge Analytica team that handled Donald Trump's presidential election campaign in the US in 2016. Amrish's name later emerged in Indian newspapers during the Cambridge Analytica controversy.[65] Following that, he continued his political

---

[62]PTI, 'Narendra Modi Urges Supporters to Take "Main Bhi Chowkidar" Pledge', *The Telegraph online*, 16 March 2019, http://tinyurl.com/5b9p48yp. Accessed on 19 February 2024.

[63]Beckett, Charlie, 'India's Digital Democracy: A Personal View from the 2019 Election Campaign Frontline', *LSE*, 5 August 2019, http://tinyurl.com/yc67ew4d. Accessed on 19 February 2024.

[64]'How BJP Used Data to Craft Landslide Win', *Hindustan Times*, 25 May 2019, http://tinyurl.com/353mfesf. Accessed 19 February 2024.

[65]'K.C. Tyagi's Son Amrish Denies Link with Cambridge Analytica, Says Firm Never Worked for JD(U)' *Outlook*, 30 March 2018, http://tinyurl.com/mwz4ymnn. Accessed on 21 February 2024.

consulting business in India. He managed a campaign for the Congress in the Himachal Pradesh by-elections in October 2021. When the results were announced on 2 November, the Congress had comfortably won the by-elections. However, Amrish joined the BJP exactly one month later. We have already seen that, since 2014, all of the consultants engaged by the BJP for elections have worked only for them. In general, these have been seen as BJP in-house consultancies. The fact that Amrish joined the BJP showed that things have progressed beyond this.[66]

The same thing happened in the Congress. When Prashant Kishor gave a presentation to the Congress senior brass in 2022 for the 2024 general elections, the entire proposal included him joining the Congress. Sunil Kanugolu was a member of the CAG that supported Gujarat CM Narendra Modi for prime ministership in 2014. He later joined ABM when I-PAC was created. Following that, he served as a consultant for the DMK and AIDMK. When things between Prashant Kishor and Congress did not work out, Sunil Kanugolu joined the Congress.[67] Following that, the Congress established a task force for the 2024 general elections, which included top Congress leaders like as P. Chidambaram, Mukul Wasnik, Jairam Ramesh, K.C. Venugopal, Ajay Maken, Priyanka Gandhi, Randeep Singh Surjewala and Sunil Kanugolu. Services of Sunil Kanugolu was also fully utilized by the Congress in the 2023 Karnataka Assembly elections, which the party won by a substantial margin.

What is the point of including them in party folds when elections can be won even through independent consultancy? According to Amrish, parties are now asking for loyal consultants. An independent consultant cannot be expected to deliver much in

[66]Interview with Amrish Tyagi

[67]Sinha, Vaishnawi, 'Who Is Sunil Kanugolu, Congress Poll Strategist Responsible for Historic Win in Telangana?', *Hindustan Times*, 3 December 2023, http://tinyurl.com/4rmef3e6. Accessed on 21 February 2024.

this regard. This is about Indian politics, where loyalty arguments do not fit very well. Politics in general has been conducted solely for mutual benefit. If there is an advantage, even a long-time foe joins a party. This occurs frequently, and in such instances, no one thinks of loyalty. The condition of loyalty just for the political consultant does not seem like a valid argument in this scenario. But whatever the case may be, this trend is obvious at the moment. If this trend continues, it is probable that some consultants will join regional and local parties in the near future.

One thing is often said about Indian politics: Rajya Sabha is the final destination for all professionals or intellectuals who join any party. The same thing was claimed about Prashant Kishor when he joined Janata Dal-United. He was appointed as an advisor to Bihar CM Nitish Kumar, and later as the party's national president. Newspapers also reported that he would be running for Lok Sabha from Buxar. However, he was kicked out of the party in January 2020. There is a good chance that some consultants may ascend the political ladder in the near future. How long will people who make others run for office be able to keep themselves from succumbing to the temptation?

This is a brief history of Indian election professionalization. Many specifics were obviously left out, but the goal here was not to provide complete details but to convey how this trend began and how far it has progressed. Even if election campaign work was secretly done on a huge scale, it was in the hands of tiny businessmen. All of this labour has evolved into an organized business over the last 15 years. Jobs that had been assigned to party think tanks have been taken over by students from IITs, IIMs and foreign colleges. Dedicated workers have been replaced by executives who were free to switch loyalties with each election.

Previously, the reins of election campaigns were in the hands of persons who were either linked with some ideology, with some leader or with people climbing the political career ladder; others also used to join the election campaign for personal reasons. This work has been taken over by people outside the party and the local political ecosystem during the age of political consulting. These technocrats, professional managers and finance specialists injected fresh tools into Indian elections.

What do these electoral consultants, technocrats and professional managers do? They create messages for the party or candidate, conduct opinion polls, do research to determine the flaws and strengths of the party and Opposition, conduct public relations, conduct grassroots campaigning and create commercials. They hold extensive focus group talks based on numerous sorts of feedback for each issue. The most significant work is data mining and data analytics, which are critical for a successful political campaign in the current era.

In today's world, a major electoral struggle is being waged on social media; this is a game in which political strategists specialize. They determine the mood of the general public and which election issues would be useful to raise through field surveys. What should be included in the party's manifesto, what pledges should party leaders make during rallies and on which matters should they remain silent—they give advice on all these sectors. They frequently advise the party on which candidate they should field and from which constituency.

Many of these things were done in elections before political consultants came into the picture, but the only thing is that political consultants do it differently and more accurately. Consider message building. Traditionally, a message from the party or candidate was drafted and then distributed to as many people as possible. However, consultants thoroughly test the message before showcasing it. A–B testing is a technique for accomplishing this. Two sorts of communications are prepared concurrently and then sent to different people. Then, it is determined which message received the best response from the people, and the message is finalized.

Any party's brief to a consultant is relatively simple: promote the party and its leader while destroying its rival. This task of annihilating the rival often becomes more important. How far can the consulting firm go with this? Does it also undertake the task of disseminating fake news? Most people in this industry claim in conversation that they do not do this themselves, but that others can. According to a consultant[68], whether you will do the job of disseminating fake news or not is dependent on the contract between you and the party. It is also claimed that parties do not require the services of a consultant company for spreading fake information because they have their own IT cell.

In one of its investigations, *The Huffington Post*[69] discovered that such companies also worked to promote fake news during elections. During the Karnataka Assembly elections in May 2018, some websites with the appearance and feel of news portals were launched. They were called *Express Bangalore, Bangalore Herald* and *Bengaluru Times.* These websites were not only disseminating various sorts of fake news, but were also releasing bogus polls conducted by fictitious agencies in which the BJP's victory was depicted. When *The Huffington Post* examined the registrar data of these websites, it discovered that they were all tied to the ABM. The ABM was in charge of the BJP's electoral campaign in that state. All of this occurred despite the fact that the BJP has a full-fledged IT cell, which is frequently in the news for spreading fake news.[70]

Political consultants are thought to have had a significant impact on party organizations. Earlier, parties used to run on the strength of their workers at the grassroots level. During election

---

[68]From a personal interview

[69]Bansal, Samarth, 'How Modi, Shah Turned a Women's NGO into a Secret Election Propaganda Machine', *Huffpost*, 4 April 2019, http://tinyurl.com/3hkmss6k. Accessed on 19 February 2024.

[70]Chaturvedi, Swati, *I Am a Troll: Inside the Secret World of the BJP's Digital Army*, Juggernaut, 2016.

campaigns, the workers enjoyed some autonomy. As a result, they found local answers to local problems. Their election participation established them as the local elite. The entire business of a political consultant takes away their autonomy. They must now follow the orders of people who are neither local nor members of the party. The most important factor is that these consultants get the approval of their top leaders. There is frequently friction between new election specialists and old party workers.

Rajesh Serupally has worked for the political consulting firm Rashtra and has extensive election management expertise. Based on his experiences, he authored an article for *The Wire*.[71] He has provided numerous examples of such conflicts in this piece. Political consultants are developing as a new kind of political elite at a time when the existing political elites are declining.

In any case, party employees and political consultants are two distinct classes. The political consultants are typically recruited from institutions such as IIT, IIM and TISS. They could have been placed elsewhere in the corporate sector if they had not entered this business, and their compensation would have been in crores of rupees. Obviously, they are paid nearly the same here as well. Not only that but there are people who have left global corporations such as McKenzie and KPMG to work in this industry. All of this has resulted in election management becoming a corporate culture.[72]

Not only has the society changed, but so has the vocabulary of elections. The combative use of language, which the corporate sector embraced years ago, is now being employed for managing elections as well. War rooms are now being built, ambush

---

[71]Serupally, Rajesh, 'Are Political Consultancies a Threat to Our Democracy?', *The Wire*, 17 June 2019, http://tinyurl.com/wb6mtw9t. Accessed on 19 February 2024.

[72]Ibid.; 'Citizens for Accountable Governance', LinkedIn, http://tinyurl.com/5jhxv6kd. Accessed on 21 February 2024.

campaigns are being carried out, carpet bombing is being done, workers have been transformed into foot soldiers, battalions are being organized, battlements are being built, snipers are being trained and stealth bombers are being deployed. Not only has the character of the electoral campaign changed, but many new facets have been added to it.

The practise of selecting candidates based on the advice of political consultants is frequently criticized. The traditional technique of selecting candidates was to solicit feedback from workers on the ground and then consider who would be most advantageous to offer the party ticket. One reality of modern Indian politics is that party organizations at the grassroots level have grown quite weak. They have been used by powerful leaders to meet their needs. Many of these leaders are also capable of influencing feedback. These circumstances have also boosted the value of political consultants. They are meant to provide objective, outside-the-box counsel free of local bias.

Another objection is that by enlisting the assistance of professionals, the parties' existing infrastructure can potentially be weakened. Rajesh Serupally emphasizes this point a lot. He says, 'Political consultancies may help win elections—but they definitely do not strengthen a party in the long run. They work like steroids, adding bursts of strength to a political party for an election – but leaving them especially vulnerable if and when they are withdrawn.'[73]

Even if we assume that political consulting is equivalent to using steroids, can any political party function without it in today's politics? It is not possible for one party to use steroids in elections while the other parties continue to use Chawanprash. As a result, practically all parties have begun to rely on steroids. Because all

---

[73]Serupally, Rajesh, 'Are Political Consultancies a Threat to Our Democracy?', *The Wire*, 17 June 2019, http://tinyurl.com/wb6mtw9t. Accessed on 19 February 2024.

parties are doing the same thing, we cannot argue that political consulting guarantees election victory.

Aside from election triumph and defeat, political consulting has evolved into a lucrative sector that is rapidly expanding. Assocham, an industry organization, published an estimate in 2014. According to this, the business was worth between ₹700 to ₹800 crore at the time. Assocham had also provided some further estimations. For example, there were more than 150 small and large election management organizations in the country at the time. Assocham stated that these experts charged between ₹1 lakh and ₹50 lakh per constituency. However, some political consultants believe that Assocham's estimations are significantly understated. Yet, they concur with Assocham that this industry is more than doubling in size every five years.[74]

I-PAC is currently the most well-known brand in this industry. It also has a lot of its splinters like ABM and Jervis. New names include Nation with NaMo, Varah and Inclusive Mind. There are also old names, such as Viplav Communication. Aside from this, Rashtriya was in charge of Chandrababu Naidu's election in Andhra Pradesh. There are also companies called Political Edge and Creativiz. Lead Tech and Janadhar India are two more examples.[75] Dilip Cherian of Perfect Relationship has also launched his own political consultancy.[76] Aside from that, there are professionals who used to work in these companies but left after learning the techniques and now take contracts for a variety of candidates. Some have started their own businesses, while others work as freelancers. India is one of the countries

[74]Sinha, Arunav, 'Political Consultancy Firms May Rake in Rs 700-800 Crore in Poll Campaign Strategy and Management: Assocham', *The Times of India*, 18 April 2014, http://tinyurl.com/3k5fvja6. Accessed on 19 February 2024.

[75]'Top Political Consulting Agency in India', *School of Politics*, 24 July 2023, http://tinyurl.com/2ak9ckmw. Accessed on 19 February 2024.

[76]Personal interview with Dilip Cherian

in the world with an excess of political parties, both large and small. However, the number of companies providing political consulting may be substantially higher. It also means that the rate of business growth is very strong, and many professionals still see enormous potential in it.

10

WHO CARES FOR ETHICS?

Politicians generally believe that you can either take care of ethics or win an election.

Elections draw out all the harmful elements of society. Every evil seems to be involved in the elections. Without black money, it is impossible to conceive Indian elections. Black money plays a significant part in victory and defeat, from misleading people to purchasing votes. Many things have improved in the last few years, yet the use of muscle power and electoral violence is still in the news every time. Also, various types of criminals contest and win elections.

We may consider lying to be a sin, but it is one of the most significant truths in electoral politics. Election lies have progressed from mere rumours to fake news as technology has advanced. Elections are marred by abuses of power and the media. There is sectarianism in elections, there are hate campaigns, there are riots and all of this creates electoral equations that decide victory and defeat.

Talking about ethics in elections is akin to throwing a pearl before a hog. But it is still critical to discuss it, to evaluate where we are deviating from the spirit of democracy (even though democracy has been established). Also, to learn what more might be done to safeguard democracy.

There are numerous issues with election ethics. These range from methods of raising funding for election expenses to toxic campaigning, voter suppression and bribery. But here, we shall limit our discussion to the ethics surrounding the business of electoral campaigns.

The Election Commission has precise guidelines about how much money a candidate can spend in elections, and how candidates must report every aspect of that expenditure. However, the expenditure indicated in the accounts is frequently less than one-hundredth of the real expenditure. As a result, there is a widespread belief that no election can be won without the use of black money. A lot of research has been conducted on the subject, with each producing a different estimate. For example, the Centre for Media Studies claimed that ₹30,000 crore were spent on the 2014 general elections.[1] According to the same institute, ₹60,000 crore were spent in the 2019 general elections.[2] That implies the cost had more than doubled in only five years. According to Dilip Cherian, 'There is no longer any limit on spending money in elections.'[3]

Has the introduction of political consulting made a difference in election spending? The major debate is whether this has reduced or expanded the use of black money. The Election Commission has not yet issued a rule requiring these entities to report how much money they have received from parties and candidates. The widespread perception is that black money plays a significant role in it. According to Shivam Shankar Singh, while black money might play a role in various expenses, white money also plays a significant role. He argues that professionals who join these consultancies on lucrative salaries would not be paid in cash, but the money would be transfered into their bank accounts. Aside

---

[1]PTI, '₹30,000 Crore to Be Spent on Lok Sabha Polls: Study', *NDTV Elections*, 16 March 2014, http://tinyurl.com/4w4beh8t. Accessed on 16 February 2024.

[2]Sarkar, Gaurav, 'India Just Spent Nearly ₹60,000 Crore on Its Election—but Does This Augur Well for Democracy?', *newslaundry*, 4 June 2019, http://tinyurl.com/24njfaur. Accessed on 16 February 2024.

[3]Interview with Dilip Cherian

from that, if you want to advertise on Facebook or YouTube, you must pay in white money exclusively.[4]

It is usually unknown who gave how much money to which consultancy and when. We have figures from the Andhra Pradesh Assembly elections in 2019. The I-PAC was employed by Jaganmohan Reddy's YSR Congress in this election. Later, the party stated that it paid I-PAC ₹37.5 crore.[5] Rashtriya worked as a consultant for the rival Telugu Desam Party in this election. Rajesh Serupally afterwards wrote a piece in *The Wire* in which he referenced some unconfirmed sources as indicating that the YSR Congress' deal was for ₹150 crore per year.[6] The Telugu Desam Party, on the other hand, accused the ruling YSR Congress government of disbursing funds from the government treasury to district-wise appointed I-PAC staff.[7] Even if we assume this allegation to be political, it is unclear how much money is spent on consulting services and how it is spent.

Every industry has its own gossip, and the consulting profession is no exception. Such gossip may be false, but they provide insight into the type of belief system at work in this industry. It is crucial to cite one such gossip from the consulting industry here. It is claimed that a particular consulting firm that worked on an election was not funded by the party, but rather by a well-known builder. We anticipate that the builder donated black or white money to the party in the conventional manner and that the party paid the agency for its services. However, it is

---

[4]Personal interview

[5]Reddy, Sudhakar U., 'YSRC Paid ₹37 Crore to IPAC for Consultancy', *The Times of India*, 16 November 2019, http://tinyurl.com/4zs7uzyz. Accessed on 16 February 2024.

[6]Serupally, Rajesh, 'Are Political Consultancies a Threat to Our Democracy?', The Wire, 17 June 2019, http://tinyurl.com/3d5ud7nv. Accessed on 16 February 2024.

[7]'Jagan Govt Diverted Rs 274 Crore Public Money to Pay Salaries of I-PAC Staff: TDP', *etv Bharat*, 4 October 2023, http://tinyurl.com/3j9rt5hv. Accessed on 21 February 2024.

said above that the builder was directly paying the agency for the service and that the agency was doing the job for the party. We don't know how much of this chatter is true, but it does highlight the reality that there is so little transparency in the business that there is plenty of room for speculation and gossip.

In the US, there is an organization called the American Association of Political Consultants. It is a trade organization representing the political consulting profession in the US. It was founded in 1969 and is now the world's largest organization of political consultants, public affairs experts and communications specialists. Its membership includes, pollsters, media consultants, campaign managers, corporate public affairs officers, professors, lobbyists, fundraisers, legislative staff and vendors. This organization has developed some guidelines for political consultants. Every year, members of the organization are required to sign this code of ethics. There is no such practise among political consultants in India. There is no discussion of ethics among them. When a candidate files a nomination to run in elections, he must also promise an oath that he will observe all the election code's laws and regulations. Political consultants, on the other hand, are not obliged by any such formal commitment.

This does not imply that everything is okay in the US. Pew Research did an extensive survey on this topic a few years ago, interviewing political consultants, leaders and senior officials. According to the 'Don't Blame Us' poll report, 42 per cent of political consultants stated that if they are given enough money, they can make even a weak candidate win.[8] Whereas 44 per cent regretted assisting a bad candidate in winning. Based on the survey, Pew Research made an interesting observation about negative campaigns:

---

[8]'Don't Blame Us', *Pew Research Center*, 17 June 1998, http://tinyurl.com/bdfw6hjv. Accessed on 16 February 2024.

> More importantly, according to consultants, negative campaigning works. Nearly all (98%) agree the news media gives more coverage to negative strategies, and 83% agree that voters respond more to negative campaigning. In fact, while many of those who see negative campaigning on the rise blame consultants themselves (37%), nearly one-in-four (24%) say 'the public' is most responsible for the change.[9]

Generally, political consultants believe that negative campaigns are like hired guns. Although the gun is used for violence, it cannot be held entirely responsible for the bloodshed. It cannot be denied that all kinds of ills existed in the election field before the consultants' involvement, but it is also true that many of these tasks are now performed in a more effective and sophisticated manner with their help.

These ethical issues are unlikely to subside in the coming days. On the contrary, they are likely to grow fast. Especially since artificial intelligence (AI) will be employed extensively in elections. Experts around the world predict that the elections in India and the US in 2024, as well as any subsequent elections, will be entirely different. This will be the first election in which AI will be deployed on a large scale. Artificial intelligence has the potential to totally transform all three of these areas: election management, campaign management and fake news. It has the ability to accelerate, magnify and add numerous additional dimensions to all election processes. If it makes data analytics function quicker or messaging more efficient, the problems that existed before will simply worsen.

One recommendation is that if any election campaign material has been generated using AI, it should be required to explicitly mention that it was created using AI. This rule can be applied to official campaign material of the party or candidate.

---

[9]Ibid.

Elections are one of the many arenas in our lives where ethics is often overlooked. But the most serious issue with politics and elections is that we have entirely given up any hope of ethics in these areas. This is what is worst for democracy.

Elections play a crucial role in upholding the integrity of the democratic process and ensuring equitable governance. The legitimacy of electoral outcomes is bolstered by ethical conduct. However, concerning issues arise when unethical practices like voter suppression, gerrymandering or manipulation of electoral processes become accepted as the new norm. Unfortunately, a disheartening aspect is the absence of discourse aimed at ensuring transparency, safeguarding privacy and fostering fairness in the electoral arena.

INDEX